STEP PARENTING
A CALL TO STAND IN THE GAP

K.L. Brooks

Copyright © 2016 by K.L. Brooks

Step Parenting
A Call to Stand in the Gap
by K.L. Brooks

Printed in the United States of America.

ISBN 9781498460484

All rights reserved solely by the author. The author guarantees all contents are original and do not infringe upon the legal rights of any other person or work. No part of this book may be reproduced in any form without the permission of the author. The views expressed in this book are not necessarily those of the publisher.

Unless otherwise indicated, Scripture quotations taken from the New King James Version (NKJV). Copyright © 1979, 1980, 1982 by Thomas Nelson, Inc. Used by permission. All rights reserved.

www.xulonpress.com

"**Step Parents:** A step parent is a truly amazing person. They made a choice to love another's child as their own."

- www.Daveswordsofwisdom.com

Dedications

I dedicate this book to my sons and daughters whom I love:

Amber Lee-Rose Brooks,

My baby "babygurl";

Brooke Lakeishia Lavid Brooks

My "Babygirl" indeed;

Morgan Lee Shields,

My baby boy;

Mario Latrell Shield,

The one who will do great things;

And also

Marcus Lamar Shields,

My eldest son undeniably.

My love for y'all is an everlasting love.

Step Parenting

To Cheryl J. Brooks who is the mother of my children, my God-given life partner and the love of my life; my help meet indeed, my road dog, my ride or die, my ever is, and ever shall be.

To my mother, Mrs. Muggie Lee Brooks, who was for many years both mother and father to me, my seven brothers and three sisters, from the time I was fifteen. This was the age at which my father, Clifton James Brooks Sr. died.

To the late Reverend Abe Williams, who was my Chief wise-man, a father figure, and a best friend forever to me for almost ten years. I am thankful that he was there for me when I needed him the most.

To Dr. Richard Allen Farmer, who is once again my Chief Wise-Man. For his love, his proven wise counsel, for his availability to me, and for his mentorship, I am truly grateful. I am appreciative all the more for his editing this, my inaugural work.

To Dr. Tony Evans, who for twenty one years has been my pastor, my counselor, my mentor, the watchman for my soul, and my Friend. I am who I am, and would not be who

Dedications

I am, were it not for his God-inserted presence and influence in and on my life.

To Jesus Christ, my Lord and my Savior forever, my Abba, my Helper, my friend eternal, the author and the finisher of my faith, my GREAT I AM. I BLESS YOU, IN YOUR GREAT NAME, AMEN!!

Table of Contents

Acknowledgments. xiii

Introduction. xvii

DECISION TIME-Counting the Cost. 23

CHOSEN- It's a Calling 31

REALITY- Not the Brady Bunch 37

NO HISTORY REPEATING - Not parenting like we were parented 47

DISCIPLINE- To spank or not to spank. 55

COMPROMISE-The Give and Take of it All. 63

COMMITMENT-Making it work. 73

PRIORITIZE-Having a Right Perspective 81

LONGEVITY-In It for the Long Haul 91

OPEN-MINDEDNESS-Other Points of View 99

HOW WILL I KNOW?–Hearing the Voice of God 139

BAGGAGE CLAIMS- Unpacking what you're working with 147

CONCLUSION- So, What Shall We Say Then? 155

FINALLY- Pray For Me Please 171

NOTES 173

Acknowledgements

I am grateful to Lorrie, my Facebook friend with whom I share 63 mutual friends. Thanks for sharing that faithful post that sparked a fire of God in me to write this book. To Dr. Richard Allen Farmer who has been teaching me the art of "smithing" words. I am too thankful to all who played also a divine role in making this project a reality. Kudos to my little sister from another mister, Nicole Raphiel. She has been a loving but persistent "boot" to me concerning this project. And many thanks to Aisha Holman, my gift from God, who gives me an opportunity to practice the things that He is teaching me. She affectionately calls me "Daddy Brooks". I am most grateful to my Lord and my Savior Jesus Christ, Who chooses to use me in spite of me, in working out this facet of His Kingdom agenda. To Dr. Sue Kavli, who as a professor at Dallas Baptist University told me that I was an excellent writer. And I believed her.

I would like to say a great big THANK YOU to all who prayed and are yet praying for this book project. I am available to speak at your church, family conference, or gathering. I can be reached by email at PastorKL01@gmail.com, or on FACE Book at KL Brooks in Dallas, Texas. You can also write me at 6719 Clarkwood Drive Dallas, Texas 75236. The effectual fervent prayer of the righteous avails much.

Introduction

Blessed To Be a Blessing

"And God is able to make all grace abound toward you, that you, always having all sufficiency in all things, may have an abundance for every good work." 2 Corinthians 9:8

When I was very young, like most people I often wondered why God would allow things to happen to me, especially bad things. I had given my life over to God at the tender age of twelve, but it would be many years before I would truly understand the full implications of such a choice. It is only now, having surpassed the half century mark, that

I am coming to understand that God favored me with the privilege of step-parenting because He had a much greater purpose in mind. I have been blessed in order that I may be a blessing. So then, right away you may get the message that the principles that I am about to share in this book is from a standpoint of one who has made Jesus Christ the Lord and Savior of his life. If you as a reader of this book have not made this life-saving and life-altering decision yet, none of this will make very much sense to you. In fact, it will be more like foolishness to you. But you can fix that. Pray this, "Lord Jesus I am a sinner and I need you to save me. Forgive me for all my sin. I accept the gift you gave me at the cross even as you died for my sin. I receive you as both my Lord and my savior. Have your way in my life. I surrender all to you. Amen." If you prayed that prayer, welcome to the family that makes an eternal difference, the family of God.

I had a talk with my baby boy a couple of years ago, among other things, about the purpose of FACEBOOK, a social medium in which both my wife and I participate. My baby boy, now in his late-twenties, is my step-son. With the age gap between us, he and I have very different ideas about just what the Facebook medium was designed for and whom. Some days prior to our talk, my son, during a visit to our home, had voiced his unsolicited opinion about Facebook's purpose and age limitations, much to his mom's and my chagrin. I put forth an effort to let him know just how shortsighted his words were, and how hurtful thoughtless words can also be.

It was on Facebook that I saw the above poster posted by a Facebook friend and my heart leaped for joy having seen it. Our family is a blended family, and with two daughters of my own, my wife and I also raised not just her baby boy, but also his two older brothers. They were nine (9), twelve (12), and fourteen (14) when I invaded their lives, and as far as step-parenting goes, I was flying blind. I had not a hint about what to do with boys, having two girls of my own, let alone boys who were a tween, a pre-teen, and a teen already. I had no clue. I had read no books on the subject matter. I had no idea whether even any books existed on the subject at the time. But I knew how to pray. So we prayed, a lot. Having raised only boys, my wife didn't have a clue about what to do with little girls who were six (6) and eleven (11) either.

We had seemingly no help on the earth. We sought no family counseling. We did, however, take advantage of the marital counseling which was made available through our local church. This was perhaps a glorious saving grace. Stepparenting took a great toll on our marriage. The repercussions were pronounced and lasting. Even to this day. We felt hopeless and alone, but God would prove Himself faithful to us.

Now, almost a decade after we encountered the 'Empty Nest Syndrome', which brought with it its own perils of life, I saw a poster honoring step parents and the Spirit of the living God instructed me to write a book about our experiences. And now, just like then, I fully trust Him for divine guidance in this matter.

As you may be able to imagine by now, this will be a very difficult task for me. My venture will necessitate my recalling, and perhaps reliving, some very painful memories. But if this book will serve the purpose of helping even one family successfully navigate the sometimes treacherous

Introduction

waters of step- parenting, then, it will be well worth reliving the anguish we have sometimes endured as a blended family.

I am well convinced that the Lord allows us all to have experiences that will at some point be useful in serving others we later encounter. This, I believe, is a large part of how God equips us to love and to serve one another. Our lives are certainly not our own. If we undeniably belong to Christ, then we will indeed give ourselves away to be used by Him. In his many experiences, Abraham, the father of our faith, was blessed by God to be a blessing to others according to the promise. As the good book says, God is indeed able to make all grace abound toward us so that we, always having all sufficiency in all things may have an abundance for every good work unto which we are called. (2 Corinthians 9:8). God's grace, which is in inexhaustible supply, equips us with whatever we need to accomplish the task that God brings to hand. Therefore whether it is through step-parenting, writing about step-parenting, or both, grace abounds for the enhancement of the lives of others to the glory of God, Amen.

1
Decision Time

Counting the Cost

28 For which of you, intending to build a tower, does not sit down first and count the cost, whether he has enough to finish it— 29 lest, after he has laid the foundation, and is not able to finish, all who see it begin to mock him, 30 saying, 'This man began to build and was not able to finish'? Luke 14-NKJV

I never did go through the process of considering what it would be like to raise children that were not my own. In the final analysis I determined that accepting their mother automatically meant accepting them. Loving their mother inevitably called for loving them as well. If fact, I do seem to recall CJ saying to me once that marrying her meant that the boys were part of the package deal. There was no question about that in my mind from the beginning, though. But on this side of the proverbial river, I would count it as wise counsel to advise anyone to count the cost of undertaking what has become for me a lifelong endeavor, and being a grandfather of four, a generational joy.

In the throes of yet another great life storm, in 1995 getting married again, let alone becoming a step-father to someone else's children was not even on my radar. I remember praying to God, "Lord, I have had one wife to die of cancer after three long years of sickness, and another who awoke one morning after four years of marriage remembering that

"...If she never changed from the way that she was, I could very easily love her forever."

she had been physically and sexually abused by her step-father many years prior, and then decided to turn our lives upside down. If this is marriage, you can keep it!" In fact, after two life- altering marriages I desperately felt a need to protect myself from the fairer sex. I had even devised what I thought was a fool-proof test to safeguard my heart from the likelihood of getting hurt by this co-worker who had become for me a patient listening ear.

I met CJ, now my wife for some seventeen years, who already had three sons, while we were co- laborers in the garden department at the local Wal-Mart in Duncanville, Texas. This was at a point in my life when I was going through a horrible and drawn out divorce and was about to be reluctantly made a single father for the second time in my very short but very difficult thirty-two years. At that point in my life, as part of being forged by fire, I had lost my forty-five year old dad to diabetes complications at the age of fifteen, survived the premature birth of my first born at the age of twenty, and buried my first wife who had died when we both were only twenty-three years old, of lymphoma cancer after three years of chemotherapy. I had somewhat successfully navigated the treacherous waters of being a twenty-three year old single dad of a three year-old baby girl, and was emotionally devastated by a really difficult second marriage, which had lasted for six long years and into which my second baby girl was both born and torn from my life. I was spent and weary and crying out to God in the midst of what seemed to be my most difficult trial yet.

"You are not God; you are not going to grow up to be God; so you may as well let God be God in every situation."
- Rev. Abe Williams

Sensing that I was getting closer and closer to CJ, I enacted my so called fool-proof plan. It involved asking her one simple question: "Do you believe that a man and a woman can be friends without becoming intimately involved with one another?" If her answer was "no" I had determined that I would run for my life and never look back. Her answer, one she says that she does not remember to this day, was a resounding, "Absolutely"! For me at the time, this meant that she was safe

Decision Time

to hang out with. Or so I thought. On our very first date to the movies, her hand touched mine and I was smitten.

After we dated for one year we decided that we would get married. I did not do the one knee marriage proposal or any such thing. We just knew that it was the best thing. We had been working together as families and involved with each other's children and we just figured that it was the next logical step to combine forces, two heads being better than one and all. Aside from the logistics, I felt that CJ was a God-sent rock of a woman. She was, "One of the most precious wonders to ever come out of Atoka, Oklahoma", to borrow a quote from my journal dated April 23, 1996. I had also made this decision about CJ: if she never changed from the way that she was, I could very easily love her forever. Then, when I endeavored to ask God should I marry her I received what for me at that time was a strange answer. He said, "You may marry whomever you wish, as long as she is a Christian." Now this answer lined up with the word of God in 2 Corinthians 6:14 where in it says, "Do not be unequally yoked together with unbelievers…", but it was strange in that I expected a "yes" or a "no" possibly with elaboration. I expected a confirmation or a non-confirmation as opposed to a "You have the choice in the matter" type of answer. But, as my chief wise man use to always say, "Remember this KL, you are not God; you are not going to grow up to be God; so you may as well let God be God in every situation." "Amen Reverend", was always my best response to that reminder.

"...Because with step parenting, just like with parenting, love is spelled T- I- M- E!"

Admittedly, there are definitely differences between parenting and step-parenting. But basically making a decision to step-parent is akin to making a decision to parent. Just like parenting, step-parenting calls for a decision to be patient, loving, dedicated, committed, and among many other things, a willingness to put in the time. Because with step parenting, just like with parenting, love is spelled T- I- M- E! When all is said and done, step-parenting is parenting with the ability to consider children no less valuable just because you may not have had

Decision Time

anything to do with the process of their birth. Children are a gift from God, period (Psalm 127), no ifs, no ands, and no buts! Step-parenting involves a decision to parent with this in mind.

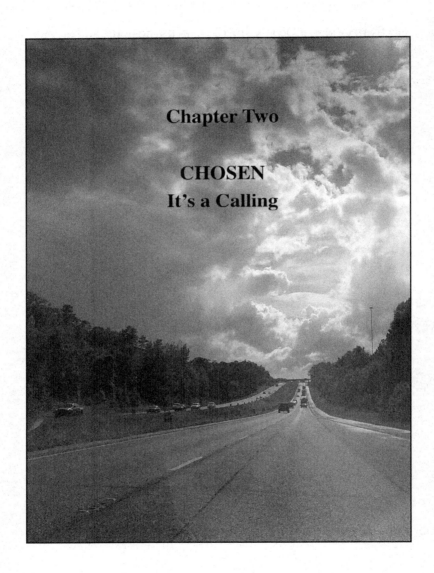

2
Chosen

It's a Calling

11 Therefore we also pray always for you that our God would count you worthy of this calling, and fulfill all the good pleasure of His goodness and the work of faith with power, 12 that the name of our Lord Jesus Christ may be glorified in you, and you in Him, according to the grace of our God and the Lord Jesus Christ. 2 Thessalonian 1 –NKJV

Though many would be the times that I would spend questioning the decision I made to take on the responsibilities of a blended family, which turned out to be one of the most difficult things I have ever done in my life, I have no regrets whatsoever. I have no doubt that this was an assignment from God created for me to take on as head of our household, husband to CJ my wife, and a father and step-father to my two daughters and to my three sons.

At one point in time when all of the kids in the house were teenagers, it felt more like "Mission Impossible"-"...Your mission, should you choose to accept it is..." I say in the house because the baby girl in the crew lived primarily with her mother in another state. She was allowed to visit somewhat sporadically, which added yet another dimension to our family dynamic. But nonetheless, again and again our faithful God, who my pastor

"...being confident of this very thing, that He who has begun a good work in you will complete it until the day of Jesus Christ;"

-Philippians 1:6 NKJV

of almost twenty years, Dr. Tony Evans declares is into multitasking, was very much on the job. He who began a good work in us would prove faithful indeed to complete it. Philippians 1:6.

Because we believed that God had orchestrated this merger of families we were free to consult Him on its every aspect. We trusted in Him with all our hearts, leaned not to our own understanding, but in all of our ways acknowledged, or consulted with Him, and He faithfully directed our path. Proverbs 3:5-6.

CJ and I saw parenting and step-parenting, even as we engaged in both simultaneously, as a call from God. It was something we could only accomplish with divine assistance, divine intervention even. Therefore, we had to make the decision that we would manage our family, and especially our children, by the book. The "Good Book" that is. Make no mistakes about it; this was a very difficult path at times. But we had to make a choice of the whole counsel of the word of God. We chose God's viewpoint over mans' or popular culture's every time. For we knew that if God created children, and God gave children as an inheritance to men and women, He then must also know all about how to raise them up. It just made sense.

I believe that when it comes to adopting children, whether it is locally or from another country, parents and or potential parents spent a greater deal of time in prayer and prayerful discussions with each other about whether it is the right thing to do. This is especially true when it comes to adopting children with special needs. For all intents and purposes, all children have a specific and special need to be loved and cared for depending on what they have gone through. And if they are in a situation where there is a need for a stand it, or step parent, be assured, they have gone through something. Thus the same qualitative and quantitative processes need be applied. We need to be sure that we are the

"For all intents and purposes, all children have a specific and special need- to be loved and cared for..."

ones precisely equipped and prepared by God to stand in that explicit gap.

We as parents and step-parents are called to be stewards over our children. We, being trusted, by God, are to guide them and steer them toward becoming Christ-centered, kingdom-minded adults before releasing them again to His care. When baby boy, the last one in the nest, had graduated from high school and was preparing for college, our prayer was similar to the one that Jesus prayed in John 17:4, "We have done what you told us to do". But little did we know that the mission was far from over. But the mission, the choice, is indeed a calling from God.

Chapter Three

REALITY
Not the Brady Brunch

3
Reality

Not the Brady Bunch

Train up a child in the way he should go,
And when he is old he will not depart from it.
-Proverbs 22:6

I had no pre-conceived notions about step-parenting before I jumped in with both feet, so to speak. But growing up in the early and late seventies the Brady Bunch TV series was the closest thing to creating a blended family and raising step children that was widely known. You remember the story of a lovely lady that was bringing up three very lovely girls, and the man named Brady who was raising three boys of his own? That was good TV, but it was not based in reality. My lady was struggling to raise not three lovely girls but three very handsome sons, and I was attempting to bring up two beautiful little girls. And that's where the similarities and or none similarities end. I don't recall what kind of work Mrs. Brady did before the union of the two families or if she even worked at all. But I do recall that Mr. Brady had a plush architect job that afforded his family a very nice house in a very nice neighborhood, and a maid named Alice.

The show had very good writers. In our reality there arose conflicts between the girls and the boys; her children versus mine. And the children did make every attempt to pit one parent against the other just like in the movie, "Yours Mine and Ours" in order to achieve a desired end- life as they once knew it. But the outcome was not always a happy ending. And it certainly did not become resolved within thirty minutes to an hour, including commercials.

In reality, step-parenting, just like parenting, is very hard work, and if marriage under so called normal circumstances, is hard work, and believe me it is, then how much more in a situation where there are multiple players both inside and outside of the home. This too is something to consider.

Outside of the home on CJ's side there were the boys' dads, an ex-husband, and sisters and brothers, who all played a role, to some degree, in what was happening in our home.

"Train up a child in the way he should go, And when he is old he will not depart from it."
-Proverbs 22:6

On the outside on my side was an ex-wife. Though we worked hard to minimize the effect of outside influences, it was a chore nonetheless. There is a particular incident that happened that I intend to include in the chapter on discipline that demonstrates this point very clearly.

In order to be an effective step-parent you must be able to see your individual family members for who they are. To be successful at that you must get to know them as individuals for whom they are. Get to know their history, their likes and dislikes. This, for me, not only included the boys, but their mother as well. I made a point of spending lots of individual time with my step sons. I asked them lots of questions. We had regular family meetings wherein we made every attempt to talk about stuff that mattered to all of us, and though I am sure that they hated every minute of it. But at least I made the effort in love to do what I believed was the right thing.

I tried to raise up my boys as the word of God says in Proverbs 22:6, "…in the way they should go." Dr. Chuck Swindoll says that the proper translation of this verse is, "According to their bent." My oldest son was somewhat athletic and set already in his ways. He was independent. My middle son was more serious and intellectual, a debate team member. And my baby boy strove very hard to be like his big brother, athletic while paying lots of

"In order to be an effective stepparent you must be able to see your individual family members for who they are. To be successful at that you must get to know them as individuals for whom they are."

attention to the young girls. Knowing their "bent", their interest, or how the Lord was shaping them, gave me somewhat of a clue about how to reach out to them. It helped me to know how to parent them.

If I may digress, even before the boys came into my home, as I began to date their mother I am sure that I came to represent to them a great change. I introduced rules into their lives that were not there before. "Clean up your room." "Whose turn is it to wash the dishes?" "Put away your video games until your homework and chores are done, please!" I never will forget the question posed by my oldest son while his mom and I were dating. He said to me, "Who are you to come around here telling us what sin is?!" I could preach a series of sermons on that question alone. But his point was well understood. Who was I indeed?

When CJ and I were wed and they all moved in with my oldest daughter, the apple of my eye, and me, I sat the boys down on the living room floor and explained the plan of salvation to them. Having finished my explanation, while sitting on the floor with them, I asked the question with my hand in the air, "Now who wants to receive Him, (Jesus)?" All three of the boys raised their hands, and right then and there, I led them in the prayer of salvation. I then urged them to select a ministry in our local church so that they would fellowship with other teens and pre-teens who believed as they had professed to. This, I told them, would prevent them from feeling like they were the only young people who lived life in Christ. Ironically, they all chose the youth choir as their ministry. And there they each served until graduation from high school. The youth workers and youth counselors at our family church were a big help to all of our children as well.

"...All three of the boys raised their hands, and right then and there, I led them in the prayer of salvation."

The truth of the matter of step-parenting is this: Children are different and have their own personalities and their own bent, if you will. It is especially important that parents discover, and then pay strict attention to how the Lord has created and is creating each child. What worked for my daughters did not work for my sons. What worked for my sons did not work for my daughters. And what worked for one son did not necessarily work for the other. I know that my oldest son must have wondered many times why I would wake him up in the middle of the night to go for walks. It was because he would give me his undivided attention during those walks like at no other time. It worked.

I was often bewildered and perplexed when it came to rearing my step sons. I tried anything and everything, so to speak. There is one thing for sure, the endeavor kept me praying. Though I had some experience raising little girls, and my daughters would tell you that I wasn't very good at that either, I had no experience raising boys. So then I had to make many desperate pleas to their Creator for help. And he did not disappoint. "If any of you lack wisdom," His word says in James chapter one verse five, "...let him ask of God who gives to all men liberally, and withhold it not; and it shall be given him." Thank you Jesus for being true to your word!

Step Parenting

In case you did not realize it yet, the so called 'Modern Family' is a crock. A family conforming to the current societal norms is nothing new or modern at all. They whole earth did it back in Noah's day, and God destroyed it, except for the lives aboard the Ark, as a result. He then set the rainbow in the sky as a sign of His promise not to destroy the earth that way ever again, not as a symbol of abominable behavior. "It won't be water but fire next time." Just as 'The Brady Bunch' television show was not based in reality in its time, nothing else Hollywood produces will work as a guide for creating and maintaining a family. It is only God who created them male and female from the beginning whose principles work together to knit together and sustain a family unit. It may indeed take a village to raise a child, but that village had better be operating under the guidance of the Holy Spirit of God the Almighty One.

"A family conforming to the current societal norms is nothing new or modern at all."

4
No History Repeating

Not parenting like we were parented

My son, hear the instruction of your father,
And do not forsake the law of your mother;
9 For they will be a graceful ornament on
your head, and chains (of honor) about your
neck.   -Proverbs 1

I recall, in the beginning of our merger, speaking to CJ about dealing with the girls or the house or both. I do not recall which. But I remember her stark reply, "I was not raised by no June Cleaver". She was making a reference to the seemingly perfect mother figure from an even older television show called "Leave it to Beaver". CJ and I were raised in totally different situations by totally different types of parents. Neither of us sought to emulate our parents' parenting styles, but to vastly improve upon them. There was friction between my father and me that I did not grasp or understand until I was twenty-five years old, ten years after he was no longer with us. There was a wall of separation between CJ's father, a stately old country gentleman, and her. He lived back in Atoka, Oklahoma and he passed away a few years after we were wed. There was a yet unexplained disharmony between CJ and her mom. She passed a few months before we were married. On the other hand, my mom, still living, and I are very close, and have been since the death of my dad. Needless to say, our parenting styles, CJ's and mine, were altogether different.

I believe and have witnessed that how we were parented as children has a profound effect on how we in turn parent children. Thus it stands to reason that how we parent our children will have a reflective effect on how we then will parent our children. I do not believe that any parent has done the job of parenting perfectly without any mistakes. There exists an added pressure in step-parenting, whether we are willing to admit it or not, of being extra careful not to "mess up" either because of a desire to impress the children, the spouse, or both. There is an innate need to be liked and accepted, but still do the best possible job as parents. I always remarked to my children that my number one priority was not to be their friend, but their parent first. Perhaps there would be lots of time in adulthood when we can be friends. Now that they are all adults and responsible for themselves, I purposely spend time working on the friendship aspect of our relationship. More often than not, my efforts are not reciprocated. Yet I am still their parent and, thus commanded by God as such to be honored and respected.

"Thus it stands to reason that how we parent our children will have a reflective effect on how we then will parent our children."

Step Parenting

I really enjoyed watching "The Cosby Show" on TV for many years. It was nice especially to see black families portrayed in a positive light on television for a change. But personally, I did not know any black families like that. In fact, I still don't. I must also admit that I have never met any black families like the one portrayed on the hit television series of old called "Good Times" either. Though the parenting skills exhibited on these shows were often foreign to me and not wholly part of my own personal methodology, I learned to appreciate them nevertheless.

My children, the boys and my girls, considered me to be an awfully strict parent, and perhaps I was. But I assured them that compared to the way my father raised my seven brothers, three sisters, and me, they didn't know the meaning of strict. I said yes a lot more often than my dad ever did. I was much more lenient than he ever was. And too, I tolerated so much more stuff from them than he ever did from us. My father, Clifton James Brooks Sr. was a no nonsense kind of guy. He wasn't just old school, he was super old school. He demanded respect, and he believed that children had a definite place where they belonged and were not allowed to stray too far from that place, if you know what I mean. I am certain that the majority of my brothers adapted a parenting style that was so much more compromising and softer than that of my dad's mainly because we felt that he was too harsh a father. I, in fact, vowed never ever to be as punitive as he.

> "...He demanded respect, and he believed that children had a definite place where they belonged and were not allowed to stray too far from that place,"

While my dad was the proverbial "hammer", my mom, Mrs. Muggie Lee Brooks was perhaps in contrast the "pillow". Don't misunderstand; she had definite standards in raising us. But I remember her being infinitely more loving and nurturing with us as a parent than my father. My father simply could not give to us what perhaps he himself was neither given nor taught. I was absolutely certain that he loved us, even as he was unable to show forth that love in normative ways. I never will forget my mom recalling to us that my dad said to her at some point in their thirty-five year marriage, "Pud'n, I told you that I loved you when I married you. Now if that ever changes I will be sure and let you know." Now that is old school to the core right? He parented the same way. I don't recall a lot of hugs, Atta boy's or any such things. Adversely, I did it, and I still do it quite often with our children.

My father, just as many other parents, did the best he could with what he had. I do not imagine that he, or my mother experienced a great deal of parenting lessons having wedded at the tender ages of fifteen and thirteen prospectively. Old school or not my dad did have a habit of kissing my mom every time he left the house. My mom said that he did that because he did not know for certain if the Lord would call him home or not before he returned. This is a habit that CJ and I have practiced for more than fifteen years now. I am sure that there is inherent in us all some good parenting qualities passed down through our parents whether we are aware of them or not. Their influence, like ours, is inevitable. But I believe that just like revelation knowledge, parenting skills can, and should be, progressive.

Chapter Five

Discipline
To Spank or not to Spank

5
Discipline

To spank or not to spank

Do not withhold correction from a child, for if you beat him with a rod, he will not die. - Proverbs 23:13 – NKLV

P lease allow me to be perfectly clear up front on this matter of spanking or not spanking. Like it or not, the word of God teaches that spanking is well in accordance with God's will concerning child rearing. Not to the point of abuse, a term which has been defined and redefined many times in our day and age; But to the point that children can feel safe and secure within the boundaries of their upbringing. The word of God says in Proverbs 22:15 that, "Foolishness is bound up in the heart of a child; the rod of correction will drive it far from him". NKJV. It therefore stands to reason that it also says in Proverbs 29:15 that, "The rod and rebuke give wisdom, but a child left to himself brings shame to his mother." Proverbs 23:13-14 says, "Do not withhold correction from a child, for if you beat him with a rod, he will not die. You shall beat him with a rod, and deliver his soul from hell" NKJV. As if that is not enough,

"Foolishness is bound up in the heart of a child; the rod of correction will drive it far from him". NKJV

Proverbs 13:24 says, "He who spares his rod hates his son, but he who loves him disciplines him promptly" NKJV. Can I get an 'Amen'?!

Now I know that for some who may have bought into this new age Dr. Spock kind of philosophy for raising children this may be a lot to swallow, but chew on it very slowly like the cow chews its cuds. It is biblical and it is in there, and in this case, Father truly does know best. Whether we are parenting or step-parenting, it does not matter; it is the whole counsel or the word of God alone that we follow. Everything else, and everyone else that does not line up is in error. "Let God be true, but every man a liar." Romans 3:4

I have five brothers-in-law and four sisters-in-law, where once there were six. I distinctly remember during our first year as a family that one of my brothers-in-law, who shall remain nameless, did something that could have been all together catastrophic. I had taught my eldest son to drive. Because he inherited or adapted a lead foot from his mother, I had to repeatedly remind him that, "The brakes are your friend!" One evening we sent him to Wendy's burgers to bring back dinner for everyone. He came back with a great big crease in the side of the family minivan from getting too close to that big bright yellow concrete filled post protecting Wendy's menu board. So, I applied the "rod of correction". Now somehow, all of my brothers and sisters-in-law found out about it. Some of them called to express their outrage at my spanking my son, their nephew. Even the brother that this side of the family only heard from about once a year, if that, chimed in.

I informed them that this was a family matter and that they were out of place. I then invited them to pay our bills, buy the boys food and clothing, then having earned a right to have a say so, call back. But until then, "butt out!" But one of my brothers-in-law took it a step further. He gave all three of my sons a pocket knife with these instructions, "If he hits either one of you ever again, stick him!" I found out about it from a confidential informant, and collected and discarded the pocket knives.

In the book of Hebrews chapter 12, the author seeks to give us a clue about how The Father of all regards discipline. He writes:

The Discipline of God

"...Or have you forgotten how good parents treat children, and that God regards you as his children?

Discipline

My dear child, don't shrug off God's discipline,
But don't be crushed by it either.
It's the child he loves that he disciplines;
The child he embraces, he also corrects.

God is educating you; that's why you must never drop out. He's treating you as dear children. This trouble you're in isn't punishment; its training, the normal experience of children. Only irresponsible parents leave children to fend for themselves. Would you prefer an irresponsible God? We respect our own parents for training and not spoiling us, so why not embrace God's training so we can truly live? While we were children, our parents did what seemed best to them. But God is doing what is best for us, training us to live God's holy best. At the time, discipline isn't much fun. It always feels like it's going against the grain. Later, of course, it pays off handsomely, for it's the well-trained who find themselves mature in their relationship with God." –The Message – Hebrews 12:5-11 Wow!!

If The LORD God, Creator of heaven and earth, disciplines His children whom He loves, should we not do the same? Not in anger, not in spite, but as we see what is best for them. Rather than exegete the aforementioned scriptures from the book of Proverbs concerning how children are to be raised or disciplined, I have selected to allow them to speak for themselves without much comment.

Now, having said that, there arises a question concerning who gets to spank, or discipline who? There is a wise man named Ron L. Deal on my favorite radio station 90.9 KCBI here in Dallas, Texas who has a ministry called Family Life Blended. This ministry is geared specifically to step families. Ron suggests that it may be best if each birth parent disciplines their own child or children, not the step parent. With this I wholeheartedly disagree. I believe that just like in a non-blended family, dad, if he is able, and with all things being equal, by default setting, if you will, needs to be the disciplinarian in the home. Now I know that I preceded that hypothesis with a number of qualifiers. And I did so on purpose. If the father and or step father in the home is not able, because of a tendency toward anger, a lack of courage, or passivity, to name a few reasons why he should not be the one to discipline, then it is incumbent upon the mom to carry out this all important responsibility. Nevertheless, I believe that FamilyLifeBlended.com is a worthwhile resource indeed. You can also see Family Life Blended on You Tube and listen online at Oneplace.com. They are also on Facebook.

Suffice to say, spanking, and other methods of discipline are not only a biblical concept, but a necessary part of parenting, thus all the more of step- parenting. Howbeit, what we do, we do in love.

Chapter Six

COMPROMISE
The Give and Take of it All

6
Compromise

The Give and Take of it All

10 Be kindly affectionate to one another with brotherly love, in honor giving preference to one another; -Romans 12 – NKJV

In a house full of growing children and growing opinions and preferences, there needed to be some bedrock foundational ideology in place that would serve as guideposts for how a family gets things done. I selected Romans 12:10 as a hallmark in our home in order to set the stage for the sometimes scary notion of compromise. Webster dictionary defines compromise as a-"settlement of differences by arbitration or by consent reached by mutual concessions; something intermediate between or blending qualities of two different things". Two different things struggling to become one, I might add. Compromise is an important and necessary concept when it comes to step or blended families. It can be a tremendously beneficial tool when used correctly.

In preparation for compromise becoming a ruling philosophy in our home I not only chose Romans 12:10 as our family's foundational base but in fact the entire chapter of Romans 12. All twenty-one verses were read and reread at family meetings and devotions as a matter of course. At one point I think that I even instructed the children to commit the chapter to memory. There are some real solid concepts in this chapter about love, mercy, grace, prayer, and consideration.

"For as we have many members in one body, but all the members do not have the same function, so we, being many, are one body in Christ, and individually members of one another."

-Romans 12:4-5

"I beseech you therefore, brethren, by the mercies of God, that you present your bodies a living sacrifice, holy, acceptable to God, which is your reasonable service. 2 And do not be conformed to this world, but be transformed by the renewing of your mind, that you may prove what is that good and acceptable and perfect will of God."

"For I say, through the grace given to me, to everyone who is among you, not to think of himself more highly than he ought to think, but to think soberly, as God has dealt to each one a measure of faith. 4 For as we have many members in one body, but all the members do not have the same function, 5 so we, being many, are one body in Christ, and individually members of one another. 6 Having then gifts differing according to the grace that is given to us, let us use them:"

"Let love be without hypocrisy. Abhor what is evil. Cling to what is good. 10 Be kindly affectionate to one another with brotherly love, in honor giving preference to one another; 11 not lagging in diligence, fervent in spirit, serving the Lord; 12 rejoicing in hope, patient in tribulation, continuing

steadfastly in prayer; 13 distributing to the needs of the saints, given to hospitality."

14 Bless those who persecute you; bless and do not curse. 15 Rejoice with those who rejoice, and weep with those who weep. 16 Be of the same mind toward one another. Do not set your mind on high things, but associate with the humble. Do not be wise in your own opinion.

17 Repay no one evil for evil. Have regard for good things in the sight of all men. 18 If it is possible, as much as depends on you, live peaceably with all men. 19 Beloved, do not avenge yourselves, but rather give place to wrath; for it is written, "Vengeance is Mine, I will repay," says the Lord. 20 Therefore

> "If your enemy is hungry, feed him;
> If he is thirsty, give him a drink;
> For in so doing you will heap coals of fire on his head."
> 21 Do not be overcome by evil, but overcome evil with good."

Yes Lord; indeed I wanted my household to eat, sleep, and breathe these words. Not just the children, but their mother and me as well. This scripture was a fitting anthem to soothe the sometimes turbulent waters of a blending family with step-children on both sides.

Now there was another scripture that carried just as much or an even greater weight in our household, one that perhaps my eldest daughter came largely to despise, and with good reason. To couple with Romans 12, I chose also Romans 15:1, *"We then that are strong ought to bear the infirmities of the weak, and not to please ourselves."* Unlike Romans 12, Romans 15:1 was not read aloud at family meetings. Neither was it required for memorization. It was only mostly discussed between my eldest daughter, who was about to be twelve years old at the time of the family expansion, and me. In our home, my daughter Brooke and I bore the brunt of this statute since I had been a Christian since the age of ten and she had been a Christian for a number of years by the time CJ and the boys joined our clan. CJ and the boys were new to living the Christian life. We therefore were "the strong" and they were "the weak". So then, when it came to compromise, we sort of received the short end of that stick on purpose.

On the lighter side of applying this concept, Brooke and I were used to having a real Christmas tree in the house for the Christmas season. I was raised in the rural areas of Mississippi. We called it "the country". And for as long as I can remember my brothers and I simply took an ax and wandered out across the pastures and cut down a Christmas tree. The aroma of real cedar was simply magical during the holidays. And this was Brooke's and my custom as well. CJ worked at Wal-Mart for a number of years, thus she and the boys were used to an imitation Christmas tree. The compromise agreed

"For everyone to whom much is given, from him much will be required; and to whom much has been committed, of him they will ask the more.
- Luke 12:48

upon was that we would have an imitation tree one year and a real tree the next. It never happened. In fact, with all of the children out of the house, it's still not happening. Enough said about that. The artificial tree yet rules our holiday season.

On the weightier side, when it came to dealing with a teenaged little girl who had become accustomed to having all of her daddy's attention, CJ was not faring too well. And asking her to imagine if her perceived anguish was multiplied by three did not help my cause. Emotions on both sides were all over the page and leaping beyond the page. I appealed to my "baby girl" based upon Romans 15, because clearly at that point she had not only been a practicing Christian the longest, but I thought she was also the most spiritually mature and yielded at the time. *"For everyone to whom much is given, from him much will be required; and to whom much has been committed, of him they will ask the more"*, Luke 12:48 NKJV. Fair or not fair, we got through it. God was then, as He is now, the God of recompense and reward. He sees to it that Romans 8:28 and 29 are always true. Everything both works together for our good, and conforms us to His image who loves Him and are called according to His purposes.

Compromise always calls for give and take. It, in my best estimation, may sometimes also call for give and give, and give. Sometimes we must ask ourselves the question of questions: "Is it worth it?" Whether the answer is a resounding yes, or a whimpering yes, the decision must then be made to do whatever it takes, even if that is the most difficult choice. 2 Peter 1:5-7 says, *"But also for this very reason;* [What reason?] *"That through these exceedingly great and precious promises you may be partakers of the divine nature , giving all diligence,* [painstakingly doing whatever it takes to get the job done], *add to your faith virtue, to virtue knowledge, to knowledge self-control, to self-control perseverance, to perseverance godliness, to godliness brotherly kindness, and to brotherly kindness* love." I could very well repeat all of that but I can in no wise say it any better. The one thing that strikes me the most concerning this matter is that we ourselves are commanded to "ADD", give all diligence, but "add to" our faith, virtue, knowledge, self-control, perseverance, godliness, brotherly kindness, and finally love. If we do this, compromise becomes easier indeed. The key to compromise after all is said and done, is perhaps a state of thinking that my beloved pastor Dr. Tony Evans likes to call, "Other mindedness".

7
Commitment

Making it work

Therefore, my beloved brethren, be steadfast, immovable, always abounding in the work of the Lord, knowing that your labor is not in vain in the Lord. - 1 Corinthians 15:58 –NKJV

My chief wise man, Reverend Abe Williams, use to joke about the fact that if his wife, Ms. Ethel ever left him he would not know it, because if she left, he was intent on going with her. He said to me one day that he entered into his marriage covenant with a self-imposed "no divorce" clause.

Step Parenting

Then, when I called upon him for clarity, he went even further to explain that he believed that as believers we really do not have a choice in the matter. And that God calls for us to work out the matter avoiding divorce as a matter of sequence. "Because", he went on to explain, "Divorce not only hurts the (offending) spouse, but the children as well; Because even if they are step-children, they are still your children, like it or not." Now that is commitment personified! Can we talk about being "steadfast" and "immovable"? This kind of wisdom is why Reverend Abe Williams was the chief of my earthly counsel under Christ for almost ten years. He passed on to glory in January of 2015, three days before my birthday. Reverend Williams raised two step-sons of his own. Thus he spoke from experience.

"God's sovereignty and free will are not at odds. In fact they coexist. For God is not just sovereign, He is sovereignly sovereign."
–Seminary Professor at DTS

There is a statement that one of my seminary professors made in class back in 2005 that instantly steadied my life which was quaking from a separation and an impending divorce. Because of my marital problems the seminary's policies required that I take a mandatory leave of absence in order to take care of the situation. I pleaded with the administration not to take from me the one part of my life that seemed to make sense. I had many questions for God and I needed answers. At the beginning of the class the professor began to speak, and it was as if he was speaking to me alone in a theater styled class room full on seminarians. Without an introduction or provocation he began to say, "God's sovereignty and "Free will" are not at odds. In fact they coexist. For God is not just sovereign, He is sovereignly sovereign." His proclamations produced in me a Charlie Brown "That's it!" moment. I needed to know how in the world could it be that I was battling the very demons of hell to obey what I thought was God's will for my life and it be turning to rubble all around me. God is sovereignly sovereign.

The beginning of that story is that things were so rough financially in those days and for years prior that my wife had decided that when baby boy graduated high school that would be her cue to abandon ship. One day I went to her job to pick her up per usual and I was told that she was gone already. In the days that followed, the death on my marriage caused my soul to cry out from a deep place within me. And I heard the sound of an inexpressible wound. For better, for worse, for richer, for poorer, in sickness and in health 'til one us died, we had both vowed to God concerning one another. Yet there we were in a time of utter brokenness. Long story short, I pursued her for one year. At the end of that year I invited her, my chief wise man and his wife to dinner. I cooked her favorite things. I gave her an ultimatum, "I need a help meet in order to accomplish the work that God has called me to do. Walk this path with me or I will be forced to find another who is willing to do so."

"You treated my boys different from how you treated your girl", she persisted. "Yes I did", as I explained once

"For better, for worse, for richer, for poorer, in sickness and in health 'til one us died, we had both vowed to God concerning one another."

more, "But only because boys are different from girls. Our boys will one day be heads of households if not heads of state. The training had to be different", I persisted.

Having heard the voice of God from my pastor, Dr. Tony Evans' mouth saying "Don't throw in the towel", I flung it sure! The uncontested divorce was both approved and finalized. I dated another. CJ did not. We remained the closest of friends. One year later CJ heard the Lord say that we belonged together. I was utterly unable to neither see, nor feel, or believe that. Before my insanity had set in, I safeguarded myself with a new chief wise man; a chief wise woman, because I was single and dating and I needed a wise woman's perspective; and a long time Christian counselor and economic chief wise man. One day soon after CJ's revelation, these three said to me without collaboration and in successive days, "The best thing for you is to reconcile with your wife." God had gotten my attention in spite of me. A few days hence we were standing in a little park in Cedar Hill, Texas saying again our wedding vows.

What is the point of this story? What am I trying to say? Here it is: A stable marriage equates to a stable family; A husband and wife must be committed to and prioritize each other under God-not their perspective children; and parenting does not stop when children go off to college or leave the nest. There are examples to be set, prayers to be prayed, and future grandchildren to spoil. The stability of our proverbial world has far reaching implications into those of our children, especially children whose world had to be mended and blended in the first place because it had been torn asunder.

Commitment: being steadfast, immovable, always abounding in this work of family that God has called us to is a must when it comes to step-parenting. Knowing that our labor as parents and step-parents will not be for naught, but will affect lives for generations to come. So hang on in there. Fight the good fight. And having done everything you can do to stand, keep standing, (Eph. 6:13-14).

Chapter Eight

PRIORITIZE
Having a Right Perspective

8
Prioritize

Having a Right Perspective

Let this mind be in you which was also in Christ Jesus, Philippians 2:5 –NKJV

It order to be successful at any given thing, it is important that we think correctly or have a right perspective concerning that thing. Therefore, in order to correctly comprehend, understand or analyze any given subject matter, it would behoove us to get God's viewpoint, or think like He thinks concerning the matter. This is the precise essence of correct prioritization, either in step-parenting or parenting and even in life itself. Having a right perspective is a key aspect. It is like starting at the beginning because that is where you are supposed to start.

I was at the end of a job interview just the other day when the chief of security asked me what were my three main priorities or goals in life. I answered him in this wise: To serve the Lord my God and savior; to serve my wife; and to serve my children and grandchildren. As men, we are commanded by God to, *"Love your wives, just as Christ also loved the church and gave Himself for her,"* –Ephesians 5:25 NKJV. But even before that, God commanded us, *"You shall love the Lord your God with all your heart, with all your soul, and with all your strength"*- Deuteronomy 6:5; Matthew 22:37 NKJV. This is God's order of hierarchy, *"But I want you to know that the head of every man is Christ, the head of woman is man, and the head of Christ is God"*, 1 Corinthians

"I want you to know that the head of every man is Christ, the head of woman is man, and the head of Christ is God."

-1 Corinthians 11:3 NKJV

11:3 NKJV. As my pastor, Dr. Tony Evans, has often explained it to the men at Oak Cliff Bible Fellowship Church, "God is the head of Christ, Christ is the head of man, and man is the head of "a" woman." Not every woman, not any woman, but a particular woman-the one God has given him to lead. "And it is only when this alignment is in place that blessings are free to flow", Dr. Evans explained.

In the fire of a battle of controversy, and they do and will come, we need to have some preset values or priorities in place that will guide us in our decision making processes that are often severely compromised by emotional flare-ups. If beforehand we know and practice that God is first and foremost in our lives. That He is the only wise and perfect One who can be trusted with such a position. And that everything else, including our wives and our children, falls below Him. We are then able to stand the tests of all times, or rather, the tests of "our" times.

I love, love, love CJ with a biblical love. But there came a point in time once, spoken of in chapter seven, when she had a major problem with not only what God has called me to do, but also how He was calling me to do it. Bible school, seminary, and plans for a full time ministry became a perceived major threat to her monetary security and life goals. There seemed to be a major incongruity stirring. I remember saying to her after she would not hear my pleading that we should follow Christ above all, "Lest we become like a group of pack mules trying to cross a wilderness without a guide", "If giving up what God has called me to do and to be is what it takes to be with you, I will do so." She wisely responded, "Don't put that on me!" Even though that was exactly what she was asking me to do, in my best estimation. In a nutshell, I stayed the course, she left, we separated, we divorced, were friends during the one year of separation and the one year of divorce, then we remarried. God was faithful to us even when we were not.

"Imitate God, therefore, in everything you do, because you are his dear children. Live a life filled with love, following the example of Christ. He loved us and offered himself as a sacrifice for us, a pleasing aroma to God."
(Ephesians 5:1, 2 NLT)

When a mom and dad have a right priority concerning Jesus the Christ- *"But seek first the kingdom of God and His righteousness…"* , everything else will be taken care of, *"and all these things will be added to you."* (Matthew 6:33, NKJV) We have to think like Jesus, act like Jesus, walk like Jesus, and talk like Jesus, *"Let this mind be in you that was also in Christ Jesus."*(Phil. 2:5 NKJV) As parents and step-parents, most importantly of all, we have to love like Jesus. Jesus was and is totally surrendered to the will of the Father. *"Imitate God, therefore, in everything you do, because you are his dear children. Live a life filled with love, following the example of Christ. He loved us and offered himself as a sacrifice for us, a pleasing aroma to God."* (Ephesians 5:1, 2 NLT)

Now that you have settled your top priority, which is God the Father through Jesus Christ, the next priority is your spouse. Not the children. Not his children, not her children, but each other. So many parents and step-parents have fallen into the trap holding their children in higher esteem than their spouse, and the family unit just ends up failing. In the book of the beginnings, Genesis, God commanded that a husband

and wife become "one flesh". Jesus said in Matthew 12:25, "Every kingdom divided against itself is brought to desolation, and every city or house divided against itself will not stand." Jesus, the foremost authority on marriage, also said in Matthew 19:6, "So then, they are no longer two but one flesh. Therefore what God has joined together, let not man separate." If we are to be one with our spouses, anything that comes between that is a hindrance to that oneness, even, and especially if that thing is your children.

Many parents with young children and or teenagers have experienced the old "pit one parent against the other" scheme. This technique was masterfully demonstrated in a movie that I recommend for every step-parent, particularly in a blending multi-child situation, called "Mine Yours and Ours". In this movie two households, one with eight military brats the other with ten multi-racial

"Act like it is so; even if it's not so; In order that it may be so; simply because God said so."

-Dr. Tony Evans

"flower power" brats were suddenly and abruptly brought together by a midnight weeding of old high school flames brought back into each other's proximity by a class reunion. One household had been accustomed to be ran by a military admiral with order and precision. The other by a very relaxed parenting style that could probably best be described as controlled chaos. When unexpectedly forced to cohabitate, the kids on both sides very quickly figured out that fighting each other was getting them nothing but in trouble with both parents. So they decided to "divide and conquer". The masterfully evil plan almost achieved its desired result.

In my ongoing experience, these diabolical patterns do not necessarily end with them becoming adults and moving out of your house. Our children are in their twenties and thirties and on their own, and we are even now dealing with divisive behavior resulting from an evil, howbeit well-meaning deceptive plot carried out against the primary relationship, our marriage. I never would have believed that what happened would ever have happened. But there we were, well into the empty nest phase of our marriage, wondering if it would even survive the decision made by a mother and her son. The family is yet experiencing a rift. But we will survive, because Jesus is Lord of our lives, and there is nothing too difficult for Him.

A worldly wise man once said to me that a woman with children ALWAYS chooses her children over any mate that comes into the picture at any later point in time. It is my firm belief that a husband and wife must prioritize one another even if the other partner does not! Concerning my marriage, a wise man quoted our pastor in his definition of faith by saying, "Act like it is so; even if it's not so; In order that it may be so; simply because God said so." In other words, even if what you believe God for is not yet your reality, by faith, behave as if it is. Dr. Evans is also often quoted as having said, "Faith is in your feet." Jesus told the ten lepers, "Go and show yourselves...", and while going, in obedience, they were healed. A mother and a father, a step mom and or a step dad and their prospective spouses; a husband and a wife-must prioritize each other first and foremost.

Chapter Nine

LONGEVITY
In it for the Long Hall

9
Longevity

In It for the Long Haul

"And let us not grow weary while doing good, for in due season we shall reap if we do not lose heart". – Galatians 6:9 –NKJV

I f you do not know, and if you have not heard, then let me be the first to inform you- parenting is a lifelong quest. It may take many different forms, or it may morph into many different stages, but I am forever my mother's son. As long as she is on the planet, she is mindful of that fact, and I must be also. In this fifty-two of her eighty-four years, she has never ceased to pray for me. She is wholly interested and fully vested in my success. All of my failures and successes will be both heartfelt and celebrated throughout her days. She will always be my Mamma, with all of the rights, privileges- and responsibilities.

And so it is with CJ and me and our sons and daughters. We live on our knees before God on behalf of our grandchildren, children, and their significant others. We sincerely desire to see them succeed and live a life in Christ with eternal rewards. Our earnest desire is to see our family perpetuate the good news of Jesus generationally until He comes again.

All of that to simply say that in my best estimation, long after children and step-children have left the nest, they are still your children. And speaking of the nest, I am all in favor of children leaving the home to test their own wings. Even as

"In my best estimation, long after children and step-children have left the nest, they are still your children."

children are a gift from God, I believe that they are a temporary gift. We as parents are to rear them to a certain age and then set them free. This normally happens at around the college age seventeen or eighteen. At that age or time, like the eagle that stirs her nest making it uncomfortable for the young ones to remain, children at that point should have been trained in the rudimentary things of God and prepared to face a world that is fundamentally adversarial to the concepts of a sovereign God who is ruler and Lord of all.

What I am not in favor of is kids moving back into the home after college. Once they are out, they need to remain out. Once they are independent, they need to seriously maintain that independence. Naturally there are exceptions to every rule. Children are different and situations should be judged on an individual basis. If they need to come home for a short time that time perhaps that time needs to be measured. Too much help can be a bad thing, and too, having been on their on for a season there will naturally be a tendency to develop habits not compatible to the longtime rules of a parent's home. Habits like sleeping until noon each day for

Step Parenting

example. Or the one that burns my britches, coming home late after the alarm has already been set. It is these types of things and other little annoying behaviors that has led my Mom to say for years, "Every grown person needs their own place."

A friend of mine, who happens to be a single mom of teenagers who are in college and high school, posted a video on Face Book depicting a young man sleeping after day break whose mom called him to wake him up. Hearing her voice he jumped straight up out of bed in an angry rage growling under his breath, "What does she want with me?!" She thought it was cute and insightful. I thought and posted, "That kid needs his own place." This also speaks volumes about the differences in parenting styles also. Some style preferences are neither right nor wrong, sometimes they are simply different. Making that statement made me want to ask for a good "amen".

My dad, Mr. Clifton J. Brooks Sr. and my mom, Mrs. Muggie Lee Brooks were married at the young gentle ages of fifteen and thirteen respectively. They bore together a total of sixteen children. Five died in miscarriages and eleven of us were raised in their home. My father was a strict disciplinarian and my mom was and is a nurturing type. They were married for thirty years before he died at the tender age of forty-five. I was fifteen years old. My mom is now eighty-two years old. At last count she has thirty-six grandchildren, thirty-seven great grandchildren, and ten great, great grandchildren. BLESS THE NAME OF JESUS!

CJ comes from a large family also. Her mom, Mrs. Callie Shields and her dad, Mr. John Shields bore seven sons and six daughters. To date there are ten grandchildren and eleven great grandchildren.

Unlike our parents, when CJ and I came together seventeen years ago, she had three boys and I had two girls. Being the sentimental one of the two of us, I suggested that we have a child together. Being in our thirties, CJ suggested that I had lost my ever loving mind. Being in love does produce brain functions that mimic insanity traits. At the ages of fifty and fifty-four, and being almost ten years into our empty nest era, we are so glad that our preliminary parenting years ore over. We are exercising the fantastic option of having the grandkids over and sending them home.

Step-parenting, like parenting, does not stop when the children reach a certain age. It simply changes forms and or dynamics. As parents, we are in this for the long haul. Both of CJ's parents are deceased. My eighty-two year old mom lives in Mississippi. For thirty-two years, since my first year in college, I have called her every Sunday mornings at six. For the last few years, I have also called her every Tuesday morning at six. Out of all of my brothers and sisters, I am the only one who has and still does, live out of state for a great number of years. If I do not call her on either of these days, I will soon get a call from another one of my brothers saying, "Mama said give her a call." We have an understanding, and I gladly comply. She is my mom after all. And that will never change.

Chapter Ten

OPEN-MINDENESS
Other Points of View

10
Open-Mindedness

Other Points of View

4 For as we have many members in one body, but all the members do not have the same function, 5 so we, being many, are one body in Christ, and individually members of one another. Romans 12, NKJV

As a step parent who does not, by any means has all of the answers, I thought it would be prudent to include other points of view. So then I invited other step mothers and step fathers to share their points of view, or testimonies if you will. Once this idea was conceived, I felt even bolder still and decided to include some points of views from other step children also, including two children of my own. It proved very interesting to hear the different experiences of my daughter, the step daughter of my wife, and my step son, the son of my wife. Though collecting these testimonials was like pulling teeth at times from all involved, I believe the idea was nevertheless inspired of God.

Guideline questions for other Step Parents:

Are you a Step Mother, or Father?
How did you come to be a step-parent?
At what stage are you in the step-parenting process?
What was your greatest challenge as a step-parent?
What is your greatest accomplishment?
What is the result/outcome of your step-parenting?
What were some questions that you wish you had the answers to when you got started?

What would be your best advice to step parents who are just getting started?

TESTIMONIALS

Cheryl B. is my wife of eighteen years altogether, and the mother and step mother of my children.

Cheryl B.'s Testimonial

Guideline questions:
Are you a step mother or father?
Step mother
How did you come to be a step-parent?
I met K.L. at Walmart, where we both worked at the time. He had two daughters and I had three sons. We dated for one year and got married in 1996.
At what stage are you in the step-parenting process?
All the children are grown, not so much hands on now, yea!
What was your greatest challenge as a step-parent?

My greatest challenge was going into something that I hadn't done before, and wouldn't do again without lots of counseling.

What is your greatest accomplishment?

The fact that we still speak to each other and not want to strangle each other is an accomplishment, right!?

What is the result/outcome of your step-parenting?

Realizing that it is a process and it is a job that shouldn't be taken lightly, and not without counseling for everyone involved, including the children.

What were some questions that you wish you had answers to when you got started?

How and when my parenting skills, and those of the other parent, meld together.

And what was the best way possible to have agreement between the two parenting styles.

What would be your best advice to step parents who are just getting started?

Listen to your children, be fair, counseling, counseling, counseling.

Joel A. is a good friend and a brother in Christ. He is married to Melanie whose testimonial follows his.

Joel A. –Step Father

I, Joel Alegnani am a father of 3 children (2 boys, and 1 girl) and became a step-dad to 5 additional youths (2 boys, and 3 girls) 5 years ago when I married my wife Melanie. At the time we married, we had 3 of our kids in high school, and the other 5 already working to support themselves. Our household in the months following the wedding was with the 3 children still finishing their high school education. As many of our dependents are over 20 years old, it is a slow process of earning the respect and bonding since daily interactions are often not possible. I believe my greatest challenge in being a step-parent has been building relationships with the young adults, not living at home. I believe my greatest accomplishment thus far for 2 of the step kids was sending them through college, and earning their respect and friendship along the way. I am hopeful, and like to think in different ways that I have positively affected their lives, and/or quality of life. Both Melanie and I were quite knowledgeable about step parenting, from studies and information we gleaned from other couples in our church, as well as Ron Deal and Focus on the Family ministries. We both knew, and accepted that as the step parent, we were the "stranger" in the house to each other's kids, and would have to hold the standard of common respect. I believe my advice to any becoming new step parents would be, that the relationship cannot be forced, and can so easily be harmed or compromised... that great diligence needs to be given to loving your new spouse primarily, and in time that love we are called to which resembles the love of Christ will be induced throughout the newly blended family – and, be patient. It is a marathon, and not a sprint.

Melanie A.

Are you a step Mother or Father?

I am a stepmom.

How did you come to be a step-parent?

Open-Mindedness

My husband and I married when we were well in our 40s. We each had teenage and older children. My husband had three kids, and I had five. Of his three, one lived with him when we married, and of my five, two lived with me. The rest were grown and living elsewhere.

At what stage are you in the step-parenting process?

We have recently moved from having no children living at home with us to now having two children (my youngest daughter and my husband's oldest son) living with us. At first, this was a strange time for me because I am more of a disciplinarian and actively guiding parent than my husband. My natural inclination would be to have quite a bit of dialog with our kids as they came back home regarding plans and our thoughts for them, such as: Are you saving money? Where do you think you would like to live when you move out? How do you plan to prepare for your move out – are you saving money toward it? When do you anticipate this to be? Do you like your job? Do you plan to stay there, etc? I believe my husband also wants to guide and groom, but his approach is much slower and far less direct than mine. In fact, very little conversation is involved with my husband's approach. With my daughter, I easily have these direct conversations, and she views them positively. But in my capacity as stepmom, I have been more hesitant. In the beginning, I felt my efforts in this direction were met with some unspoken disapproval from my husband. I even found it difficult to approach the subject with him due to the tension the subject seemed to cause between us. There were times when I felt my husband didn't "have my back" in certain matters, being more protector to his son than partner to me. For the most part, I believe these times were more misunderstandings – the kind that the Enemy easily exaggerates in an effort to destroy a marriage. As time has progressed, this tension has subsided, and my stepson and I have had many of these conversations. This was after much prayer. I learned to pull back on my way of having one conversation that discusses many things, and learned to use a bit of my husband's approach of having small, three-or-four-sentence conversations here and there. Since this is what his children grew up with, I realized I had to meet them where they were more comfortable. Bit by bit, I am able to have more detailed conversations – still somewhat pulled back, but a little more satisfying for me now.

What was your greatest challenge as a step-parent?

Probably the greatest challenge as a stepparent I have had is, as I have mentioned before, I see discipline and teaching and dialog as loving guidance, and my husband seems to see this more as overly invasive. I feel that my children have benefited greatly from the way I raised them, and I feel his kids have missed out because they haven't had this kind of intentional interaction with a parent. All of my kids call me from time to time for advice or my view on things. I have felt such frustration because I felt that we had been missing the mark with his children. I am realizing now that perhaps my husband has had this approach because that is what his kids respond to. I have felt very frustrated because I have felt that what I naturally bring to the table as a parent was being quashed by disapproval. This challenge put a strain on our marriage as it became an issue we didn't even know how to discuss with each other as husband and wife.

What is your greatest accomplishment?

Through prayer, God brought to my attention the need to follow my husband's lead with his kids, but adding my own bit of flavor. Basically, a change in my attitude of frustration and disapproval of my husband's parenting has been my greatest accomplishment. I had always felt that one of my stepsons liked me a lot. I easily had good conversations with him. I also felt that my stepdaughter appreciated me and has always been glad that her dad has me in his life. And now I have developed a good relationship with his son that recently moved back in with us. All of our children have seen my husband and me go through very difficult times within our marriage. They have seen some bad times in this marriage. Yet they have been able to see our faith and our desire to follow the Lord and our respect for marriage, due to the Lord's respect for marriage, cause us to stay together and fight to make our marriage work. Therefore, another accomplishment has been demonstrating that marriage is worth fighting for.

What is the result/outcome of your step-parenting?

I feel that parents are parents forever, so I think the outcome of parenting is ongoing for a lifetime.

What were some questions that you wish you had the answers to when you got started?

I wish my husband and I had discussed so much more beforehand. Since some of our children were grown and the rest near grown, we were able to get away with the difficulties of our parenting differences. I believe with younger children it is much more important to be on the same page because there are so many parenting decisions on a day-to-day basis. We just should have talked "what if" scenarios out so that we had an idea ahead of time as to what our agreements or compromises would be. So much happened soon after our marriage which caused sudden changes for our children and where they lived; namely, my father-in-law's death. There was no time to discuss how we would handle things since it was a sudden change under the weight of a tragic loss. Some beforehand discussion of "what if" planning could have helped us as we had to make some on-the-spot decisions.

What would be your best advice to step parents who are just getting started?

If you are about to marry, and there are older children involved, discuss what role each parent expects the other to play. Discuss parenting boundaries that both agree on, such as what kinds of decisions can be made individually by a parent and what decisions must be talked over first. Think of as many "what if" scenarios as possible and have a rough idea of the expectations of these scenarios. Having said that, however, remember that being flexible is also necessary. Even the best pre-made plans may not actually execute well or feel right when an actual event happens, so if your spouse needs you to be somewhat flexible, try to be that for them just as you would hope they would be for you. Remember that "love never fails" (Corinthian 13:8), so if you will parent, step-parent, and spouse (be a mate) out of true faithful love (even if at times the only love you "feel" or respect is your love for God), then God will make everything okay – eventually! Also, no matter how old children get, they are the children of their mother and father, so allow them that relationship for all their lives. Equally remember that the job of a parent is to raise good citizens, faithful disciples, future spouses, and future parents to function well in the world, so share that goal together!

Jemeica A. is my niece. She is one of several dozen and one of my favorites. She is married to Mendez, my favorite nephew-in-law, whose testimonial follows hers. Together, they are one of my favorite couples.

JEMEICA A. –Stepmother.

I became a stepmother when I married a man that had 1 daughter. I am in a place of guidance for this child. She is an adult now and only requires advice and resource for day to day tasks. My greatest task as a step-parent was discipline issues. My spouse and I were reared differently and he had instilled the same in her. My greatest accomplishment regarding step-parenting her was getting my step daughter to graduate high school. The result of my step-parenting has been having her still rely on me for life lessons and spiritual concerns. One of the biggest questions I wish I had asked is "what do you (speaking of my spouse) want from me" being the female in the house with this child? My advice to beginners: 1) Decide before hand on discipline tactics, 2) Find out their views on discipline, 3) Decide on money matters regarding the child and the other biological parent, 4) Date longer!, 5) Discuss spiritual practices and beliefs, 6) Start a savings early!

MENDEZ A. –Step Father

I am a step-father. I became a step father when I married a woman that had a son. I am able now to give him advice on girls, having a relationship with God and helping him establish his goals. My greatest task has been realizing that my wife and her son's father have known each other for a long time. Her comfortableness with him and his family has caused issues. My greatest accomplishment has been developing a friendship with the step son. One question I wish I had asked is, "how do you spend your money when you get paid"? I wasn't into the church when we started dating; my wife gave financially and spiritually and I was not used to that! My advice to those step parents just starting out is, give it all to God!

Mario P. is a good friend and a brother in Christ. He once was a member of OCBF church also. His mother, another good friend, still is a member.

MARIO P.

My name is Mario Price – a first-time husband of five years, a one-time single father of a 20-year old son and a stepfather of an 11-year old daughter. I am part of what is called a blended family. While raising my teenage son as a single dad, I met a beautiful young lady through eHarmony who was raising her then 5-year old daughter.

Early in the courtship, we realized that the relationship would be serious and decided to introduce the kids to the mix with a family date night. I realized that if my wife and I were going to have a harmonious relationship with each other, we would have to have healthy harmonious relationships with our children. After a 6-month courtship we became engaged and four months later we were married and all living under one roof.

One of the greatest challenges that we have faced is the blending of parenting styles and traditions. Both my wife and I came in with expectations of what is the "right" and "wrong" way to do things, as well as what we expected to be "normal" parenting roles and rules. Although these differences often caused stress and some aggravations, we worked through this with prayer, communication and remembering that love brought us together.

Gregory M. is a friend of a friend and a brother in Christ. He is also a member of OCBF Church in Dallas, Texas.

GREGORY M- Step Father

A Step-Father's perspective

When I met my children's mother she had four (4) pre-existing children; ages 3, 9, 11 and 12; three boys and their older sister. Their mother and I didn't really "date", but actually started a serious courtship a few months after meeting. We married a year and a half later but my co-parenting role had long since been established. Throughout the stages of our courting I had taken on responsibilities for the children in a number of aspects from meeting the children before and after school, helping with homework and school projects to picking them up from school and meeting with teachers. At the time I had no flesh and blood children of my own so I became wholly committed to my roles as a family man well before we even discussed marriage. The greatest challenges initially were my son- who was extremely spiteful, upset at the fact that his mother had previously moved on from the twelve year tumultuous relationship she'd been in with his father.

What I didn't realize at the time was the depth and severity of a relationship over a twelve year span proliferated with violent physical and emotional abuse, drug and alcohol abuse; hints of sexual abuse; police and child protection services interventions and homelessness. Some things were revealed to me upfront; others, over time. Nevertheless, I committed to her and the children and never considered myself a "stepparent". The two biological fathers of the four children were not involved in their lives and that was a complication that we did not have to deal with, but what became an issue for us was discipline. There was not much of it in the beginning of the courtship, but as my time with the children increased my presence appeared to be more accepted over time initially by our youngest son at the time, who took it upon himself to call me "Daddy" very early on, despite the ridicule he received from one of his brothers. Where the problem came was in how their mother dealt with discipline issues. She had a non-confrontational approach to certain things in the beginning. She would see things and hear things, but would not actively engage the children. I would often mistakenly step up and address issues of concern and attempt to resolve them. I was not at all diplomatic and my tactics –intended to correct the issues- often created more situations. I had a military background and had recently completed a police academy, but I had a great deal of difficulty tailoring my approach to meet their specific needs. What I couldn't seem to grasp was the individual child's needs and how to effectively reach each child individually. In other words, I had a difficult time establishing a one on one relationship of trust and discipline with each child with exception of the youngest boy. What began to happen was a series of mishaps because the adults involved made critical errors in the development of this very un-blended family. As time went by I foolishly and often confided my concerns to my immediate family, that being my mother, father, sister, grandmother and my best friend. Whenever my wife and I had a disagreement that didn't get resolved I would often consult one of them. This was a mistake in many cases as most of the situations were over my handling of household affairs concerning the children. As I stated, my wife was often selectively non-confrontational and often allowed me to step into things and then chastise me afterwards. I would not have been so taken aback by this had it not been for the fact that she often chastised me in front of the children and quite often before even addressing the children for their behaviors or other contributions to the issue at hand. By confiding in my family and not resolving the issues in my own home first, I inadvertently helped create misgivings between my family, my wife and the children. Another concern that manifested itself later in the marriage- after we added two more children to the household —was that due to some unfulfilled needs my wife had with my relationship with the oldest children, she never fully identified the children collectively as our children. She to this day has always referred to them as "her" children. It didn't seem to matter what I did for them, with them or on their behalf, I was never accepted by her as their fully fledged father. I often felt like the third wheel, like I was just sharing space and giving of myself. Over time I built up quite a bit of resentment. And unfortunately it manifested itself in my attitude towards the oldest children and my wife. My mother-in-law and years later my sister-in-law moved in with us. My oldest son and then daughter-along with her daughter had moved out and back in- eventually our granddaughter lived with us for some time- but I learned quickly that in-laws does not mean "allies" in the family when it comes to tactics instituted by the children when they had their own agendas. So fast forwarding ten years; a lot of detail I cannot go in to as it would be a book in itself, but to say the least , what did I learn from this experience? For the unmarried, but considering a ready-made family; first and foremost, remember that it is exactly that; a pre-existing family... with a history. Be very careful whom you allow to interact with your children. Observe and ask questions that call for an elaborative response when gauging the relationships. Watch for signs of divisive tactics from the children, but remember you are either the inside biological parent or the outside "step-parent" and you must establish and respect certain boundaries in the beginning. Develop healthy relationships between the children and the new parent- and any involved biological parent not in your household- and certainly before adding additional biological children to the mix. Agree on who and how you will discipline in your home. Above all, begin with God, His Christ and the Holy Spirit in your relationship form the beginning. Everything hinges on the relationship that is built on this foundation. The enemy comes to steal and destroy and especially the family. A Godless broken and dysfunctional home often produces a broken family of people that struggle hopelessly, but a broken family brought together under God that chooses to be decisively indivisible from God's authority is much more likely to produce prosperously. Unfortunately, my household suffered because I failed to heed the true calling on my life as the spiritual head of the household. I attempted to helm a damaged ship without God, Christ and the Holy Spirit as my compass and guide and ran the ship aground, eventually scuttling it. MEN: Your calling is to be the spiritual head of your home and family, not the final authority. God is the designer, orchestrator, the director, the producer and the property master of these productions which we call ours that have gone astray, I am reminded that my job isn't finished. My oldest three children are grown and living their lives. I recognize that I need God and with the Lord's constant help I am learning to better help my youngest three find their way in this world and set them up for their individual mission fields. Families, He must be the opening and finale in them. blended family is God's ultimate ministry field. Like the Church, it is made up of people from all walks of life and backgrounds. In my opinion a blended family is a broken family to begin with, but one of spiritually grounded individuals can be a success testimony even if just one member shares their faith and lives in such a way that others see their struggle and the faith that walked them through it and comes to Christ. This is where I am today. Though I struggle almost daily with thoughts of a failed marriage, and children, I stand.

STEP CHILDREN TESTIMONIALS

Guideline questions for step children

How old were you when blending began?

Did you resist a change?

What was it like joining families?

How did you feel about your new siblings?

How did/do you feel about your new step parent?

What did you think about their parenting style?

What did other blood siblings think?

What kind of relationship have you had with step parent since leaving the home?

What kind of relationship do you now have with that step parent?

What kind of relationship do you plan to have in the future?

What are you doing to facilitate that relationship?

What do you wish that your step parent would have done differently?

Brooke Brooks is my elder daughter and the apple of my eye. She is a sister in Christ, a Jesus lover, a missionary who once traveled eleven countries in eleven months with Adventures In Missions, and spent seven days on mission in Cuba before relocating to California to help with a church plant. She is special indeed. And I am so proud of her. She is, and will always be, my 'Babygurl'.

Brooke LaKeishia Lavid Brooks – Step Daughter

This account is only from my perspective and since my perspective is a human one, things are naturally skewed.

My blended family journey started in 1996. I was twelve years old and itching for a new mom. I was first introduced to Ms. Cheryl by my dad of course. She was pretty to me with long black hair. At the time, the only relationship I remembered having with a mother wasn't a good one. During the interim after my father's divorce, I remember asking God for a new mom. I had some fanciful expectations based on the families I saw on TV, which you'll later see proved detrimental. I was excited to meet her but was very cautious. I remembered the last mommy dad had brought home and I also remembered the blows to my rib cage, she'd sporadically take when angry. Those memories were vivid in my mind then as I nervously wondered what this new relationship would bring. I was an emotionally tormented little girl looking for approval. I think I was the most excited about starting our new family. I remember my teenage brothers rolling their eyes as I bounced around with excitement. Now, let's be clear. I had my dad for almost two years to myself. I had become spoiled with his time and attention. I soaked it up the best I could, being that in the previous marriage he worked all the time and ministered all of the remaining time. Now that I had him to myself, I only wanted to share in small amounts. I'm sure my brothers picked up on this. It was evident in how they treated me.

During the honeymoon phase of my father's engagement, things with my potential step mother were great. I was excited and doe-eyed that this one would prove advantageous for me. In my mind, I was finally getting the mother I wanted. She took me to the salon for the first time in my life, I rattled off a million questions, a million miles a minute, and I was super excited. She seemed laid back and really didn't get angry much, which was a breath of fresh air considering that was polar opposite from my last step mother. Also, my father's parenting style was way strict. At the time, I didn't know what my sister thought of her. She was living with my previous step mom. Things were crazy over in that camp. But I was excited and hopeful concerning the new one that was taking form for me.

I remember when Ms. Cheryl had come home from marrying my dad. I ran up to her beaming and said something to the effect of "Welcome home mom!" She sneered at me and said something to the effect "Get away from me." Don't quote me. I may have gotten the exact words wrong but I can still feel the sting to this day. I don't think I've felt an emotional pain like that ever again. It took my breath way and confused me. I went to my room in a daze and vowed to never let her in. I did that with the last one and I could write my own book about how that turned out, but I won't, for now. After that moment, I noticed a change in her. The rejection was carried out in our day to day interaction. I felt invisible and unwanted. Needless to say, I tried to get my dad to see who she really was and that started a string of competing for his time, pointing out petty occurrences, frustrated arguments, loneliness and bouts of depression. That pretty much summed up our relationship until I went away to college.

When I left the house I felt rejected. I don't know what it's like to be a step parent but I'd like to think she did the best she could with where she was.by my entire family. I didn't feel my brothers cared, my step mother basically acted as if I wasn't there and my father had taken her side in all of this. Dramatic, I know. I get it honestly. Since then, the relationship has been pretty nonexistent; cordial and peaceful but nonexistent nonetheless. Over the last few months, I've been praying about what I'd like the relationship with my future children and step mother to look like and I've been working on trying to cultivate that now. First, I'd like to finally have a relationship. Not the fairy tale, family matters, step by step relationship I selfishly wanted as a kid. No, a meet you where you are and love you for the package you are in type of relationship. I'm no longer looking for her to fill a void only fillable by Christ himself.

Having been healed from the baggage of my childhood and walking in continued healing, I don't wish of Ms. Cheryl anything different than what happened. I don't.

Mario S. is my middle son. He is about two years younger than his older brother Marcus, and about two years older than his younger brother Morgan. He is astute, witty, ambitious, and full of faith. He is my brother in Christ. He is also a member of OCBF Church here in Dallas, Texas. The last time I checked, Mario is working at least three jobs, one full time, one part time, and one entrepreneurial with Amway. He is also involved on a seasonal basis with judging high school debates. I am so very proud of him. Through all of the adversities that have come into his life, he is yet striving to overcome. And with God's help, I have no doubt that he will.

Step son-Mario S.'s Testimonial

1. **How old were you when blending began?**
   a. First blended marriage 7/8yrs old,(going into the 2nd grade).The second time I was 14 in the (8th grade)
2. **Did you resist the change?** Second marriage we resisted.
   a. **Why?** Because we had already had to deal with being uprooted from our home and routine. And also, we watched how our Mom, who was basically the only constant my two brothers and I knew at that point had to struggle on her own, the pain it brought upon her, and how hard she had to work to get by as a single parent.
   b. **Why not?** I didn't the first time because it was exciting and new and we were all enthusiastic about a new beginning. There was some apprehension about moving from small town Oklahoma

to big city Dallas/ Fort Worth but that was only due to our laid back conservative personalities.

3. **What was it like joining families?**

   a. There is always an adjustment because everyone comes from a different way of doing things and personality types/flaws

4. **How did you feel about your new siblings?**

   During the first experience the other stepsisters were living with another parent, and too, already out of the house with a family of their own.

   In the second experience I was neutral, or ok with until my stepsisters disrespected my mother. It appeared to me that my brothers and I were forced into being respectful at all times while my new sister could do no wrong.

5. **How did/do you feel about your new step parent?**

   a. I did feel some resentment because of areas where I felt there was hypocrisy at the time. That being said, I was a stubborn teenager so I know I had my faults as well.

6. **What did you think about their parenting style?**

   a. I think at the time it was unfair and unyielding but one to the takeaways, almost like Jiminy Cricket's voice of conscience, "Life is about choices", has had a tremendous impact on my life. Although I didn't get it at the time, I do realize that God placed my PG, (Parent Guardian-step father), at a pivotal time in mine and my brother's lives to give us a mental toughness that honestly wasn't something readily available in our family at that time, or perhaps even to this day.

   b. I realize that, one, life is hard, and two, being a black man has its own set of challenges so little lessons about "fleeing from the appearance of evil", and, "don't fall into the trap of what others think because they don't feed, shelter, or clothe you," are thoughts that flash across the battlefield of my mind as a banner to help strengthen and comfort me in times of despair or weakness.

7. **What did other blood siblings think?**

a. We were at various stages of adolescent development. So thoughts and effective communication of these thoughts was a work in progress. This was one of my areas that I have to work on at the time also.

8. **What do you wish that your step parent would have done differently?**

    a. I wish that I would have gotten more validation for my interests, debate, reading, music/theater and more "nerdy" pursuits. Because confidence has always been difficult, especially around other males. There was always doubt and questions as to am I good enough or masculine enough. I'm naturally softer spoken and introverted until a blowout from repressed anger or whatnot in the past. So I have had to learn how to speak up, and out, and to vent a lot of pressure and stresses in my life.

b. emotions were in a constant upheaval, (or flux). There was a lot of distrust, anger, and tension. But we fought through it.

9. **What kind of relationship have you had with step parent since leaving the home?**

    a. We had several phases of peace and other times of conflict. But (I believe) that is natural in all relationships, especially if there is to be trust and growth. There has to be space to be transparent. Even God lets us come to him in happiness, sadness, pain, gladness, and anger. I mean we as humans have some emotional crisis at times.

10. **What kind of relationship do you now have with that step parent?**

    a. I feel that there is mutual level of respect and understanding. We could be closer, but that takes time. Unfortunately life doesn't make it easy what with work and distractions. But I know that we will keep building.

11. What kind of relationship do you plan to have in the future?

    a. I would hope that the goal is honesty and trust. In life, especially among men, "Iron must sharpen Iron". So hopefully we can have that type of balance.

12. What are you doing to facilitate that relationship?

Nicole R. is my 'little sister from another Mister' indeed. I am so grateful for her pushing me to finish this book project. It was Nicole who, when once I was speaking out loud about my heartache over never being able to inspire the boys to reciprocate my long suffering attempts to bond with them, said to me, "Don't you know that your presence in their lives reminds them of their birth fathers who abandoned them in life?" You could have knocked me over with a feather. When I was single for a short while, Nicole served as my chief wise woman. I appointed her as such because I knew nothing about being single, dating, nor a single woman's point of view. She served me well in that capacity. And I am forever grateful.

NICOLE R. –A Step Daughter

1. **How old were you and your natural siblings when the blending began?** Answer 1: I was 10 years old when my mother and step-father married.

2. **Did you resist the change? Why? Why not?**

    Answer 2: As a child you have no choice in the matter. Therefore, I did not resist. However, the awkwardness I felt lasted for years. There was no point to resisting the change, since it was going to occur with or without my acceptance.

3. **What was it like joining families?**

    Answer 3: It felt like consonantly having a guest in the house. In other words, awkward. Nonetheless, my mother's siblings, aunts and uncles accepted my step-dad without question. Therefore the transition wasn't notable.

4. **How did you feel about your new siblings?**

    Answer 4: He did not have any children to blend. I am glad I didn't have to deal with birth order issues.

I was the only child for a year until my brother was born. I've never considered him as a half-bother. Just brother.

5. How did you feel about your new step parent?

Answer 5: I had to go the process of learning him. Overall, I'd say that I was indifferent once I got past the awkwardness. My step-dad's a very easy going man which helped me through the process.

6. What did you think about their parenting style?

Answer 6: My mother took care of the heavy lifting when it came to me. My step-dad relied on her for the parenting.

7. What did your other blood siblings think?

Answer 7: N/A

8. What kind of relationship have you had with your step parent since you left their home?

Answer 8: As an adult, I have a healthy respect for him and his wisdom. As a child, I thought as a child. As an adult, I understand his love for me in the form that he gives it.

Step Parenting

9. What kind or relationship do you have now with your step parent?

Answer 9: Our relationship today is very healthy. The awkwardness has finally left. We can now talk about anything.

10. What kind of relationship do you hope to have in the future?

Answer 10: A continued healthy and loving relationship

11. What are you doing to facilitate that relationship?

Answer 11: I've maintained healthy communication with him.

12. What would you wish that your step parent would have done differently?

Answer 12: **The cha**nge I wish that would have taken place perhaps would have been for me as a step child to have been allowed to walk with my Mom and step dad early on, after the proposal. This I feel would have allowed me time to process and understand what was about to happen. I believe that once you decide to marry another with children, that you marry the children as well. I needed time to put this new relationship in a place so that I could have fully embraced my new family member and understand my place in my mother's heart sooner than later.

Chapter Eleven

HOW WILL I KNOW?
Hearing the Voice of God

11
How Will I Know?

Hearing the Voice of God

"My sheep hear my voice, and I know them, and they follow me..." John 10:27

J ust like all of the successful endeavors of our lives that we venture to undertake, step parenting has to be God appointed, and therefore, God anointed. I have a cousin who pastors a great church in Philadelphia, Pennsylvania who used to be a running back for the Philadelphia Eagles back in the seventies. He said to me once that there are two kinds of people who pastor a church- "The called, and a fool."

"Because", he said, "Only a fool would take upon himself that which he is not called to do." He went on to explain that when a man or a woman takes upon themselves a role that God has not called them to, they are on their own, without His power to accomplish the task. God's anointing is God's power made available to do God's will. This power to do is made available when the child of God is who, what, when, where, and how God Himself is calling them to do and be. My pastor/cousin gave up professional football in order to pastor the church to which he was called.

So then, how in the world are we supposed to know if the proverbial gap that we find ourselves facing is

"How do we discern the voice of God for His direction and clarity concerning such a life altering decision that may affect so many lives so indelibly?"

indeed the gap in which we are called specifically by God to stand in? How do we determine that the 'mission' at hand -and it is for all practical purposes, undeniably our personal mission? How do we discern the voice of God for His direction and clarity concerning such a life altering decision that may affect so many lives so indelibly?

There are both practical and spiritual answers to these questions. Because while "God is Spirit", He also instructs his children to be both spiritually and practically wise. The general wisdom, or God's general will, Dr. Tony Evans always say, is found in the word of God, the Bible. His wisdom pertaining specifically to our own individual situations,(illumination), or God's specific will, comes through the Holy Spirit because of a personal relationship with the Father via His Son.

Jesus said in John 10:27, "My sheep hear My voice, and I know them, and they follow Me." Wow, what a magnanimous statement by the awesome Good Shepherd. "My sheep, the ones who belong to me, the ones for whom I am totally responsible. The ones I purchased with my own blood; the ones whom with great love and patience I personally lead, guide, and direct- My sheep." "These are the ones who hear my voice even as I speak. These are the ones with whom I am intimately acquainted. I know them. And because they are my sheep; and because they hear My voice; and because I AM familiar with them, even with My family; They know what to do and where and when to go- They FOLLOW Me." (NKJV).

Ephesians 2:10 states that we are God's 'workmanship', Masterpiece, the New Living Translation says: His Poeima in the Greek, His (*personal*) poem; "Created in Christ Jesus for good works, which God prepared beforehand that we should walk in them." This scripture informs us that King David was absolutely correct in his writings in Psalm 139:16 wherein he writes, "Thank you for making me so wonderfully complex! Your workmanship is marvelous—how well I know it. You watched me as I was being formed in utter seclusion, as I was woven together in the dark of the womb. You saw me before I was born. Every day of my life was recorded in your book every moment was laid out before a single day had passed." In other words, God has so planned, orchestrated,

"All means all, and that's what all means."
-Dr. Sony Acho

and predestined our lives that we would be foolish indeed not to check with Him in order to follow the plan that He has predestined for us to follow. Now, in His sovereign pre-planning He does, without a doubt along with that gives us free choice and free will. But He knows the plans that He has for us. They are good plans, and we can and must trust them, even as we trust Him who reserves the right to alter or change our plans altogether.

My cousin in Philadelphia, who is also a pastor, once told that he believed that God sovereignly allows, and restricts what he wills to happen in the lives of His children, particularly as it relates to marriage. And if God makes restrictions in marriage, then how much more does He makes them in the family? God created family. We must remember that God is not only sovereign, but He is sovereignly sovereign. This means that He is not only in control of everything, but that He rules and reigns over everything and everyone that exists. "The earth is the Lord's and the fullness thereof, the world. And they that dwell therein," Psalms 24:1 declares. Colossians chapter one verse sixteen declares that all things, (including the family), were made for Him, through Him, and to Him, speaking of Christ. Pastor Sonny Acho used to proclaim to us, "All means all, and that's what all means." John 1:1-3 says that, "In the beginning was the Word, and the Word was with God, and the Word was God. He was in the beginning with God. All things were made by Him, and without Him nothing was made that was made." It is all about the One who created family. And since He created family, should He not be consulted concerning the families He creates? God commands believers to seek Him concerning all things. Proverbs 3:5, 6 says, "Trust in the Lord with all your heart; lean not to your own understanding. In all your ways acknowledge, (consult with) Him. And He shall direct your path." And all means all; and that's what all means.

So, how will you know if the assignment before you is your assignment? How will you know that you are called to take up or answer the call of building a family unit together with the ones with whom you have become familiar? He will tell you. Just ask Him in prayer, and perhaps fasting would be very much in order for such a momentous decision. And if the two of you "agree on earth as touching anything that you shall ask," it will be done for you by God the Father. Matthew 18:19. KJV. My best advice to you is this, practice hearing His voice. Prayer is just a two way conversation with the LORD of the universe. Therefore, when you pray, be sure and take some time out for listening after you have spoken. God has much He wants to say back to you.

Chapter Twelve

BAGGAGE CLAIMS
Unpacking What You're Working With

12
Baggage Claims

Unpacking What You're Working With

7 Husbands, likewise, dwell with them with understanding, giving honor to the wife, as to the weaker vessel, and as being heirs together of the grace of life, that your prayers may not be hindered. **-1 Peter 3**

Have you ever heard the story of the wicked step mother who was very abusive to the point of attempting to murder her step daughter? Or have you heard tell of the evil step father who was a heroin addict who caused the drug dealers to come to the home of his new family seeking payment for the drugs he consumed on credit? Of course you haven't. How much do we really know the people with whom we fall in love with at a moment in time when best feet are put forward and both of you are on your best behavior? How much can we get to know the person who by nature instinctively puts on a mask in order to conceal the flaws or even the human frailties of a person on a mission to capture the hearts of their targeted beloved? I don't really know any definitive answers to these questions, but allow me to make a case that it would be well worth your time to make every effort and try.

Dr. Tony Evans has often reminded the men, as well as the congregation, at Oak Cliff Bible Fellowship Church, and through his radio and television ministries, the world, that when we marry a man or a woman we marry all that they were, all that they are, and all

"When we marry a man or a woman we marry all that they are, and all that they were"

-Dr. Tony Evans

that they are becoming. All that they were includes all of the hurts, pains, and abuses that they have endured. This, unfortunately or fortunately, depending on your point of view, also includes all of the ill effects and or strengths derived from said experiences. We all respond in one of two ways to the things, and the people that happen to us in life- we either fight, or we take flight; we stand firm, or we cower; we allow it to do great harm, or we allow it to make us stronger. For the sake of argument from those who felt as if they had no choice in the outcome real or imagined, I remind you that this book is written based on Christian principles. That being said, Romans 8:28-29, a familiar verse of scripture tells us this, *"And we know that all things work together for good to those who love God, to those who are the called according to His purpose. For whom He foreknew, He also predestined to be conformed to the image of His Son, that He might be the firstborn among many brethren."* That is to say that when we love God and are called according to His purposes, number one, all things must work together for our good, and "all means all". And these things, at the same time, will cause us to be conformed to the image of Jesus Christ His son, or to make us more like Him. My Mom would often put it like this, "That which does not kill you, will only serve to make you stronger." But I digress. My point is, when we marry, we marry a person's history, good and bad and ugly; their family and family history, good and bad and ugly; and what those people, places and things has caused them to become, or not.

When we marry a person's history, everything Mother and Father did and or did not do, their brothers and sisters, their cousins, their nieces and nephews, their childhood bullies from the playground, all of that can very well follow them into the family and household that you are trying to build together and become a factor, and a hindrance, or even an unwanted part of the family dynamic. It is hard enough to try and merge into one, a man from Mars and a woman from Venus, so to

"…all of that can very well follow them into the family and household that you are trying to build together and become a factor, and a hindrance, or even an unwanted part of the family dynamic.

speak. Let alone dealing with the hurts and the pains of their collective pasts. It is also noteworthy to mention that, depending on the ages of the child or children, they may also have experiences or hurts that may affect their abilities to relate to other family members. Remember the mentioning of the "Wicked step mother" in the beginning of this chapter? When my daughter was four years old, that person entered her little life. Remember the mentioning of the "Evil step father"? That person entered into the life of my wife and my three step sons a few years before I came onto the scene of their lives. We all brought suitcases of hurt into the family unit we were trying to create together. And these suitcases of hurt had, and are having a profound effect on each individual in our family conglomerate. These suitcases can, and in most cases will, have a devastating effect on any family unit. If this is true, or rather, since this is true, would it not behoove us to learn as much as we can about a potential spouse and their child or children pre matrimonially, or on the north side of the proverbial broom as humanly possible? Now, with all of that being said, there is good news, even very good news, in

Step Parenting

the midst of all of this theoretically uninviting news. There is a local pastor named Jimmy Evans here in Dallas, Texas who has a ministry with his wife Karen called Marriage Today. Jimmy preached a sermon call, "The Hurt Pocket". In this sermon on marriage, he recounted a story from his own life about the emotional and physical pain that his father inflicted upon him as a young boy. Having tripped over his father's feet while carrying out the garbage he triggered a violent reaction from his father. His father's response scarred him potentially for life. In fact, it affected his relationship with his wife even years later. Until one faithful day when the Lord said to him," Give Me your trash can." Having done so, Jimmy was healed from that scarring event from years past.

And that is the good news; you too can be healed from your past. 2 Corinthians 5:17 says, "If anyone be in Christ, he is a

"If anyone be in Christ, he is a new creation; old things have passed away; behold, all things are become new."
-2 Corinthians 5:17

new creation; old things have passed away; behold, all things are become new." Now as the old Baptist preacher would say, "If that doesn't make you want to shout, perhaps your wood is wet." Hallelujah!

Nevertheless, in this world in which we live, even with all things being equal, we are not all the same. We heal at different times and at different rates. It could very well be that that potential spouse, or even the one to whom you are already married may have some issues from their past. And as we have discovered, even the child or children may have some significant issues affecting their ability to relate. As much as you can, unpack those suitcases and have some frank and honest discussions about what the matters may be. Because even when we are healed from past hurts, the fact that things happened may very well, and most likely will, have an influence on how we see what we see. So, husbands, live with your wives according to knowledge as the Apostle Peter instructed. Make a case study of her. And you women do likewise. As a wise man once said, "Knowing is half the battle."

Conclusion

So What Shall We Say Then?

Those from among you shall build the old waste places; you shall raise up the foundations of many generations; And you shall be called the Repairer of the Breach, The Restorer of Streets to in which to dwell.–**Isaiah 58:12**

Decision time-Counting the cost: To all of the single mothers and fathers, more single mothers than fathers, who at some point in time may be faced with the decision of inviting someone else into your family dynamic in order to fill the all-important role of your significant other, this I say.

Pray without ceasing, investigate and scrutinize with spiritual discernment, and by all means, count the cost. Count the cost financially. Wisely consider the financial ramifications of the union. Count the cost emotionally. Consider what kind of affect the union will have on the existing family structure and dynamic. Will it make it better for the greater part? And most of all, count the cost spiritually. Is this man or woman that you are interested in already living a life that shows forth their love for Jesus the Christ, our Lord and our God? Make carefully your decisions being what the Apostle Paul called in Titus chapter two, "sober minded". Also, be very careful, if you are dating, not to introduce every person to your children, especially if you have not yet deemed them to be someone that you are serious enough about to marry. This will minimize the possibility of added confusion and stress to your children, depending on their ages.

Chosen- It's a calling: There are several questions you need to consider when facing a situation where the possibility of becoming a step parent exists. Perhaps the first one should be, are you equipped or gifted to handle this life-altering responsibility? Am I called by God to take on and love, as if they were my own, a child or children that are not my own? Do I have the right stuff? And, what is the right stuff? And if the answer is yes to all of these questions, then the particular question is," is this situation the one for me?" Now in my own situation, I loved CJ, and there was no doubt in my mind that this meant loving her three boys as well. But her clarifying question to me was; "Now you know that marrying me means also marrying my boys also don't you?" And I knew exactly what she was inferring. Having served as a member of Oak Cliff Bible Fellowship church for more than twenty-one years, I have understood again and again that we marry the person, their family dynamic and history, and everything else that makes them who they are, word to the wise. Just like all of the successful endeavors of our lives that we venture to undertake, step parenting has to be God appointed, and therefore, God anointed.

Reality- not the Brady Bunch: Reality checks are wonderful, particularly when it comes to making decisions that will have a profound effect on your life and the lives of those who you love. These types of decisions are best made with 'eyes wide open'. It is not good to romanticize a life situation based on what we may see on television or even in the movies. I will be the first to remind anyone that according to word of God, we walk by faith and not by sight, 2 Corinthians 5:7. And too, one of my favorite biblical promises that says, "You can pray for anything, and if you have faith, you will receive it.", Matthew 21:22 NLT. Not to mention the thousands of other promises found throughout scripture. But, the reality of living the Christian life calls for us to consider how the supreme LORD of the universe operates. He is the consummate Father who knows best. His answers to prayer are yes, no, and not yet, based upon His power, authority, and knowledge of everything past, present and future. Dr. Evans likes to say that He is the only one with a panoramic view. And please don't get me started about His longsuffering. That's a whole other book by itself. So yes, dream big, plan well, and work your plan. But give place to the One who knows the plans He has for you. He was the one who promised us that in this world we will have trouble, but take heart. He also promised that He has overcome the world- reality checked.

No History Repeating- Not parenting like we were parented: For almost as long as I can remember, my eldest daughter Brooke has been a little flip at the lip so to speak. Maybe even from the time she learned to speak. For years I have semi-jokingly said to her, "If I had spoken to my father like you sometimes speak to me, you would have never been born, because he would have killed me and buried me in the back yard." My daughter has always had a problem with parental boundaries. Even now, some thirty plus years later, she still feels and speaks to me often as if she is my equal. I have three years of seminary at Dallas Theological; two Bachelors of Biblical Studies degrees, one in Business and another in Christian Ministries; and a Masters in Global Leadership with an emphasis in Missions. And yet, when she and I have theological discussions about anything, she believes that her non-degreed opinion or biblical knowledge is as vast and valid as my own. I have often felt the need to remind her that I have been on the planet twice as long as she has to boot. I don't even think that the fact that I have been rightly dividing the word of truth some thirty years next year makes a difference. But I am getting a little bit better at loving and appreciating her for who she is. As for my father, I don't believe he would have tolerated the behavior even in the slightest. This fact, however, is a constant reminder and evidence that not only I, but my brother as well, made a conscious decision not to parent as we were parented, in particular where my father's parenting style was concerned. I have hopeful expectations that my sons' and daughters' parenting skills will grossly exceed my own and those of their mother/step mother.

Discipline- To Spank or not to Spank: There are many factors involved in making a decision on whether to discipline your children by spanking or not. The word of God is clear; if you love them you will spank them. But what is the age range where spanking will do the most good? What are other methods of discipline that may work with your children? When they push against the guidelines, because of the foolishness that is bounded up in their hearts, set for the safety and peace of the family, and make no mistake about it, they will push, what do you do? What can be done to maintain and restore order and or tranquility in the household or family dynamic? Know this, in a society, a family without rules and regulations there will be disorder. Passivity is not an option. You are responsible for being your children's parent first and foremost, not their friend. But remember this, "Rules without relationship will not work", says Dr. Tony Evans. And to this I am a living witness. But neither will a household without rules or consequences for bad behavior. "Be willing to let your child experience a reasonable amount of pain or inconvenience when he behaves irresponsibly," wrote Dr. James Dobson in his book-"The New Dare to Discipline". Just like parenting, step parenting is not for the faint at heart.

Compromise-The Give and Take of it all: Let me be perfectly clear, compromise is not a concept to be feared. But rather it is a bedrock principle for any attempt to blend a family. As good and as solid as the idea is, it still takes a consensus between the two governing parties, the parents, to make it work successfully. One of my oldest and wisest mentors in the ministry Dr. S. L. Spann, who is now in glory with the Lord, once said to me, "Reverend, it takes two." It does indeed take two parties who are willing to give up something now in order to reap a benefit later. Without that willingness, the concept of selfishness is present and any idea of fairness climbs out of the proverbial window.

Commitment-Making it Work: I heard a story on YouTube not long ago about a young man who informed a "Success Guru" that he wanted to be successful also. So the guru instructed him to meet him at the beach the next morning at five a.m. After some strong objections to the early hour the young man agreed. The next morning as the young man approached the meeting place dressed for success, the guru was waiting for him. The guru forthwith informed the young man that he would have no need of his nice sports coat, nice new shirt, or his brand new power tie. After he removed them the guru instructed the young man to follow him into the ocean. "Oh no", the young man protested. "I cannot swim." "If you truly want to be successful, you must follow me", the guru insisted. And so he did. Into the ocean they went; knee

Conclusion

deep, then waist deep, and very soon the water was up to the young man's chin and he stopped. "This is crazy", the young man yelled out. "I'm going back to shore." Just as he turned to go back the guru grabbed him by the head and pushed it under water. The young man thought, "He's trying to kill me. I will just hold my breath." Fifteen seconds passed then thirty, then a full minute. At that the young man could no longer hold his breath thus he began to fight for what he thought was his very life. Back at the shore the young man asked the question of the guru, "Have you lost your mind?" "No I have not," the guru exclaimed. "You told me that you wanted to be successful. Now when you want success as badly as you wanted to breathe at that moment in time, only then will success be yours." What is the point of this story? What am I trying to say? When it comes to success in any endeavor, especially step parenting, you've 'gotta' want it badly enough. Commitment is a decision. You have to want to make it work. Once you are in, you have to be all in. "No turning back; no turning back."

Prioritize-Having a Right Perspective: What is the most important thing to you in your life today? I hope and pray that the answer is Jesus Christ the maker and creator of all. But after Him, who? Or perhaps a better question would be what? When I was in seminary and struggling with life as my marriage was under attack, I was told by a young pastor that God came first, then my marriage, and then my ministry. I found this to be very sound advice. In a blended family, just as in a regular family, the husband and the wife must prioritize each other first after God, and then the children. I know-that's a hard one, especially for a mother from whose loins this one came. But, when God instructed man and woman to "leave and cleave" in Genesis two, the order was to become "one flesh" with one another. Since then we are instructed to abandon the greater, our parents, how much more our children when it comes to each other? They are not at all, no matter how hard they try, to be allowed to be a hindrance or a stumbling block to the primary relationship in the family unit. "What therefore God has joined together, let no man,(woman nor child), put asunder." Prioritizing one another creates a unified front. Division of the proverbial house more often than not begins like it began in the original garden. And a house divided against its self cannot stand. Jesus said in Matthew 12:25, "It shall not stand." A right perspective is like super glue in a step family.

Longevity-In it for the Long Haul: I do believe that divorce in America has exceeded fifty present both in and outside of the church. We simply as a society do not practice staying together as our forefathers and foremothers did. It would seem that the now infamous 1975 lyrics of Paul Simon song- "Just slip out the back Jack; Make a new plan Stan; You don't need to be coy Roy-just set yourself free", was a communal battle cry. There must be at least, "Fifty ways to leave your lover", indeed. On the other hand, we must be much more compelled to take the advice of James Ingram's 1981 song, "One Hundred Ways". Some of his advice was, "Compliment what she does; Send her roses, just because; if it's violins she loves, let them play. Dedicate her favorite song her favorite song; and hold her closer, all night long; Love her today; Find one hundred ways." Oh my, my, my, my, my-the memories that flood my soul. My point is, staying is a decision that must be made as often as necessary. Whether one hundred ways or one thousand reasons, "…Be ye steadfast, immoveable, always abounding in the work of the Lord; knowing that your labor, your toil, (of step parenting), in the Lord, shall not be in vain." 1 Corinthians 15:58. In the Baptist church growing up down in Mississippi we sang a song whose lyrics read, "Let Jesus lead you; Let Jesus lead you: Let Jesus lead you, all the way; All the way from earth to heaven; Let Jesus lead you, all the way." The word of God declares, "…being confident of this very thing, that He who began a good work in you will be faithful to complete it until the day of Jesus Christ." Philippians 1:6. So hang on in there, for "Longevity has its place." -Martin Luther King Jr. No matter how old they get, your son or your daughter will always be you son or your daughter.

Open-Mindedness Other Points of View:–"No man is an island we can be found; no man is an island let your guard down; You don't have to fight me, I am for you; We're not meant to live this life alone."-Tenth Avenue North, "No man

Conclusion

is an Island". I am convinced that no person has all of the answers. God created us for community, to live and exist with one another, to encourage one another. This, I believe is the main purpose of the church of the living God. And this is why I included this chapter in the book. We are as unique as our own finger prints, but the similarities in our individual situations may serve as encouragement for someone else. Our victories, and our struggles, may serve as assurance that our God and Father, who has no respect of person, will faithfully do for another what He has done for the one. Our testimonies, just like those of the saints of old, may serve as a witness to God's great love and care for us in our every exertion. "We will overcome, by the blood of the Lamb and the words of our testimony." –Jeremy Camp, "Overcome". Glean, if you will, from the points of views of not just these written here, but anyone that you come across who are walking this walk of step parenting. Bless yourself.

How Will I Know?–Hearing the Voice of God: Jesus said in John 10:27, "My sheep hear my voice, and I know them, and they follow me." I heard a story that back in Israel a few thousand years ago when two of more shepherd's flocks became intermingled at one place such as a watering well, the shepherd, after the sheep had drunk would walk out a short distance and call to his sheep. Recognizing his familiar voice, all that was his would follow him. Jesus said, "My sheep", the ones who belong to him; "hear my voice" the voice that is familiar because of practice; "I know them", because of a personal relationship; "and they follow me", they follow the one who knows the good plan that he has for them. Step parenting caused me, out of necessity, to pray often. I needed to hear from Him. I needed his specific instructions in the midst of my specific situations. Even more than that, I needed to know before I took on the assignment of raising children no born to me that this assignment was indeed my assignment predestined of Him. Know this beloved; every assignment is not your assignment. How will you know which is? Check with the shepherd. His appointments for you are divine. "For God so loved the world, that He gave His only begotten son; so that whosoever believes in His shall not perish, but have everlasting life." John 3:16.

Conclusion

Baggage Claims-Unpacking what you're Working with: There was a commercial that aired on all of the local TV stations some years ago whose theme was, "The More you Know". If I recall correctly, it was an ad campaign aired on behalf of teachers seeking to educate parents. The point of the ad was that the more we know about any given subject, the better equipped we would be to better handle any situations that would arise. After Peter instructs us to live with our wives according to knowledge, making it our life long goals to continually learn who she is and how we can better serve her, he then instructs us as men to live together with our wives as heirs of the grace of life so that our prayers may not be hindered. That is to say that doing so will have an intense outcome on our prayer lives. Get to know one another. Unpack the suitcases you all may be carrying. Know what you are working with. The more you know, the greater the potential for success in the matter of building a family together.

One more thing, always be mindful of the fact that there is no such thing as a perfect parent. So then there is certainly no such thing as a perfect step parent. Therefore, allow space to make mistakes, make forgiveness a guidepost in your family's modus operandi, and keep on pressing forward. And by all means, extend this same courtesy to your mate and your children. It may very well be that, "Your greatest contribution to the kingdom of God may not be something you do, but someone you raise." –Andy Stanley. Allowing God to have the final word, "A good *man* leaves an inheritance to his children's children…" Prov.13:22

FINALLY

Please Pray For Me

²Continue earnestly in prayer, being vigilant in it with thanksgiving; ³meanwhile praying also for us, that God would open to us a door for the word, to speak the mystery of Christ, for which I am also in chains, ⁴that I may make it manifest, as I ought to speak.

-Colossians 4

NOTES

Dobson, James-The New Dare to Discipline Tyndale Momentum Publishing, 1996

www.Family Life Blended.com Ron Dale

www.Tony Evans .org Tony Evans

www.Daveswordsofwisdom.com

www.MarriageToday.com, Jimmy Evans

All chapter cloud photos, as well as the back and front covers, are original cell pictures by the author K. L. Brooks

All scriptural quotes are from the New King James Version of the Bible unless otherwise noted.

K. L. Brooks is available to speak at your church, family conference, or gathering. He can be reached by email at PastorKL01@gmail.com, or on FACE Book at KL Brooks in Dallas, Texas. You can also write him at 6719 Clarkwood Drive Dallas, Texas 75236

CPSIA information can be obtained
at www.ICGtesting.com
Printed in the USA
FSOW04n0148180216
17052FS